RALPH ELLISON

Author of
Invisible Man

RALPH ELLISON
Author of
Invisible Man

Martha E. Rhynes

MORGAN
REYNOLDS
PUBLISHING
Greensboro, North Carolina

WORLD WRITERS

CHARLES DICKENS

JANE AUSTEN

STEPHEN KING

RALPH ELLISON

ROBERT FROST

RALPH ELLISON: AUTHOR OF *INVISIBLE MAN*

Copyright © 2006 by Martha E. Rhynes

Library of Congress Cataloging-in-Publication Data

Rhynes, Martha E., 1929-
    Ralph Ellison : author of Invisible man / Martha E. Rhynes.— 1st ed.
      p. cm.
Includes bibliographical references and index.
    ISBN-13: 978-1-931798-69-3 (lib. bdg.)
    ISBN-10: 1-931798-69-9 (lib. bdg.)
    1. Ellison, Ralph—Juvenile literature. 2. Novelists, American—20th
century—Biography—Juvenile literature. 3. African American
novelists—Biography—Juvenile literature. I. Title.
    PS3555.L625Z873 2006
    818'.5409—dc22

                  2005019492

Printed in the United States of America
First Edition

To members of the OWLS book club

CONTENTS

Ralph Ellison. (AP Photo)

One
COLD OKLAHOMA NEGRO EYE

During his junior year at Tuskegee Institute in Alabama, Ralph Waldo Ellison grew dissatisfied with the classes he had to take to earn a degree in music. Although he had perfected mechanical skills on his trumpet and mastered the school's classical repertoire, he missed the freedom and spontaneity of blues and jazz played in jam sessions and dance halls back in Deep Deuce, his old neighborhood in Oklahoma City.

From childhood into his teens, Ralph's primary interest had been music. Family and friends had encouraged him. After he returned home from his part-time jobs, he practiced endless scales, patriotic marches, and popular dance tunes, loud enough to drown out the noise of railroad freight cars being switched on nearby tracks.

The growing town of Oklahoma City as it looked in the early part of the century when Ralph Ellison was born. (Library of Congress)

He later admitted that when he practiced double- and triple-tonguing the notes on his trumpet, it probably sounded like "a jackass hiccupping off a big meal of briars."

At Avery Chapel African Methodist Episcopal (AME) Church in Oklahoma City, Ralph had played gospel music and traditional hymns with the church's praise band. He had participated in every music class that Frederick Douglass School offered, including music appreciation, orchestra, and marching band. He even assisted a local dentist by playing Schubert's "Serenade" on his trumpet to mask the sound of the drill when a patient was nervous. At bedtime, he played "Taps" to honor his dead father and express a "farewell to day and a love song to life and a peace-be-with-you to all the dead and dying."

Before coming to Tuskegee, music had been central to Ralph's life. Now that was changing. The more traditional music he played at Tuskegee did not touch his soul. If this was what a career in music would be like, he was no longer convinced that teaching music or playing the trumpet professionally could express his thoughts and emotions. He kept thinking of *The Waste Land,* a book-length poem by T. S. Eliot. It was written like a jazz concert, with a central theme and uneven, syncopated rhythmic passages and breaks. Its lines were packed with symbolism, clever metaphors, and repetitious sounds. The idea of writing something like that intrigued him.

After his junior year, Ellison headed north to spend the summer in New York City, where he hoped to earn enough money to pay for his final year of school. But instead of returning to school and becoming a musician, he became a writer of essays and the author of a famous novel, *Invisible Man.*

When he was born on March 1, 1914, Ralph Waldo Ellison's parents, Lewis and Ida (Brownie) Milsap Ellison, named their son after the great American philosopher Ralph Waldo Emerson, who wrote essays extolling individualism and self-reliance. Young Ralph disliked his name because the other children teased him and called him Waldo.

Ida Ellison was a slim beauty born to a family of sharecroppers on a Georgia cotton plantation. Ralph's father, Lewis Ellison, had left Abbeville, South Carolina, as a teenager and joined the 25th United States Colored Infantry, one of the few vocations, other than laborer or servant, open to African Americans at the time. Lewis hoped to serve his country in Cuba during the Spanish-American War, but after basic training he was stationed at frontier outposts in the West. In 1899, his company was shipped overseas to help subdue a rebellion in the Philippines. Lewis was recovering from a bout of malaria and dysentery when an officer ordered him and other members of his company to drill in the hot sun on the parade ground as punishment for gambling. Lewis refused and was dishonorably discharged from the military, losing his severance pay, pension, and other benefits.

After returning to the States, Lewis Ellison operated a candy kitchen and restaurant in Abbeville and worked as a foreman on a construction crew in Chattanooga, Tennessee. Then an army buddy told him about opportunities for people of color in the new state of Oklahoma.

Decades before, the United States government had removed Native Americans from the eastern states to what they called the Oklahoma Indian Territory. Many of the tribes forced to move owned slaves and took them along. When the slaves were freed, those living in the Oklahoma Indian Territory were allotted tribal land. They also established several all-black towns.

In 1889, the U.S. government decided to open up unassigned land in the Oklahoma Indian Territory for settlement. Hundreds of people of all races staked claims and towns sprang up overnight. Until 1896, male citizens in the Oklahoma Indian Territory, regardless of race, had voting privileges. However, many of the white

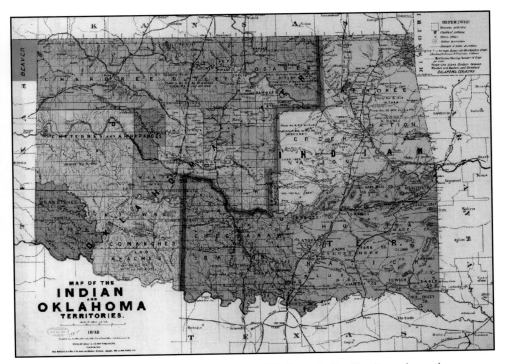

This late-nineteenth-century map of the Oklahoma Indian Territory shows the area's division into tribal lands. (Library of Congress)

leaders who flooded into the territory were from the South, where segregation was the norm. Soon it was standard in Oklahoma, too. Racism got a boost from the 1896 Supreme Court decision in *Plessy v. Ferguson,* which ruled that segregation was legal.

When the Oklahoma Indian Territory became the forty-sixth state in 1907, writers of the Oklahoma State Constitution made racial segregation a state law. The constitution also established a literacy test at the polls designed to keep people of color from being able to vote, but this was repealed in 1917. Still, Oklahoma offered a promise of escape from the worst of the segregation that had ruled the Ellisons' lives in South Carolina and Tennessee. It was a faint hope, but enough to convince Lewis and Ida to move west.

At the time of Ralph's birth, the Ellisons lived in a boarding house owned by one of Ida's relatives. Jefferson Davis (J. D.) Randolph had arrived in the Oklahoma Territory from Tennessee before 1891. Literate and politically astute, he owned a drugstore and real estate on Second Street, also known as Deep Deuce, a segregated neighborhood in Oklahoma City. Later, J. D. became custodian of the law library at the state capitol. He served as Ralph's surrogate grandfather and had great influence on his development.

Lewis Ellison worked as foreman on a paving crew until he had saved enough money to open an ice and coal delivery business and move his family into their own home. The future looked promising: Ida was expecting another baby. Three-year-old Ralph adored his father, and in return, Lewis delighted in watching Ralph amuse family and friends as he sang the song "Chocolate to the Bone." He also taught Ralph a hip-swiveling jazz step, the "Eagle Rock."

Ralph often accompanied Lewis in the wagon when he made deliveries. Tragically, on one of these trips the boy witnessed the accident that killed his thirty-nine-year-old father. While Lewis was carrying a large block of ice with tongs, he slipped and fell, causing an internal hemorrhage. An abscess formed on his liver. He lay near death in the hospital for a month. When a surgeon attempted to mend the damage, Lewis died from complications.

Ralph never forgot those last moments with his father, watching attendants wheel Lewis away on a hospital gurney. For years, he fantasized that someday his father would come striding down the street and rejoin the family circle.

After her husband's death, Ida faced poverty and depended upon friends, including the Randolphs. Lewis's body lay in the morgue until she could borrow enough money for his burial. As soon as she recovered from baby Herbert's birth, she began supporting herself and her two sons by working as a hotel maid.

The family moved ten times to avoid bill collectors, and though he was just a child, Ralph became Herbert's caretaker, a duty he detested. Herbert had a passive, dependent personality. He stuttered so badly that Ralph had to translate for him. Other children teased and bullied Herbert, which forced Ralph to defend him.

When Ida Ellison became church custodian at Avery Chapel AME Church, a center of religious, social, and political activities, the Ellisons moved into the vacant parsonage, which had a small library. There, five-year-old Ralph learned to read the books and encyclopedias that helped him create a rich internal life.

In the alley behind the parsonage, Ralph found a discarded camera lens, which in his imagination became the barrel of a cannon or a portal into a different world. Ida wanted to encourage her studious, imaginative boy.

She scrimped and saved to buy him a child's rolltop desk and a toy typewriter for Christmas.

When Ralph became an adult, he wrote two short stories based on real events that occurred during his childhood. In hopes of teaching baby chicks to fly freely like other birds, the main character in "That I Had Wings" ties tiny parachutes on them and drops them off the roof of a shed. Of course, the chicks cannot fly, and he gets into trouble. In real life, Ralph and Herbert were punished for a similar escapade.

In "Boy on a Train," the main character accompanies his mother and brother to McAlester, Oklahoma, where the mother has a new job. Because of segregation, she and the boys must ride in the baggage car, crowded with boxes, luggage, a coffin, and a barking dog. The boy can only watch as a white vendor harasses his mother, making lewd comments and using racial slurs. The job in McAlester doesn't materialize, and, like the real-life Ellisons, the family returns to Oklahoma City. This memory was a painful one for Ellison, reminding him just how alone in the world he and his little family were. In the years to come, he would often return to these difficult memories for his stories, turning them into powerful fiction.

In 1919, Ralph watched Bryant Elementary School being built across the street from his house. He looked forward to enrolling in first grade in the new school and could not understand why his mother had enrolled him instead at Frederick Douglass School, eight blocks from his home. The segregation laws seemed strange to him.

Each day Ralph walked to school down an alley, over a viaduct that crossed the railroad tracks, down brick-paved streets, between busy warehouses and loading docks, and through the red-light district, past saloons and gambling dens.

Ida warned him not to talk to strangers, but Ralph witnessed many startling scenes on the way to school and saw forbidden words scrawled on buildings. On the playground, he and his classmates jumped rope and chanted rhymes in defiance of Jim Crow segregation: "These white folks think / They are so fine / But their raggedy drawers / Stink just like mine!"

In 1921, the Ellisons traveled to Ohio to live with Ida's brother and his family for a brief time. While they were gone, a race riot occurred in Tulsa, Oklahoma, home to 15,000 African Americans. Racial tensions were high after a black youth allegedly assaulted a white woman in an elevator. Some said he grasped her arm; others claimed he raped her. A white mob threatened to lynch him.

African-American men tried to protect their property when the vandalism and looting began in the Green-wood neighborhood, home to many of Tulsa's black-owned businesses. Before it was over, white rioters had burned buildings in a thirty-five block area. Many black residents were killed. The governor had to call out National Guard troops to control the situation.

When the Ellisons returned to Oklahoma City after

Smoke from the Tulsa riot fires of 1921 fills the city's skyline. The Tulsa race riot would make a lasting impression on Ellison, who would later study and write about this event in his exploration of the history of race riots in America. (Oklahoma Historical Society)

the riot, they found the 12,000 black residents there deeply disturbed and wary of provoking racial incidents. Ida got a job as custodian at an apartment complex in a middle-class, white neighborhood. The Ellisons lived in the servants' quarters. Although they had to be cautious about their presence in a white neighborhood, the job had advantages. Ida brought home leftover food from residents' apartments and discarded magazines for Ralph to read while he baby-sat Herbert.

She also took the boys for Sunday walks into upscale neighborhoods, where homes and yards were large and well-kept. She wanted them to see how affluent white people lived. The experience made Ralph want to live in a "world in which you wore your Sunday clothes [every day]."

Ida dared to take the boys to the zoo, even though the

facility was whites-only. They entered the gates behind a group of white people, and no one questioned their right to be there. Ralph and Herbert spent an enjoyable afternoon looking at the exotic animals. At closing time, an angry guard stopped them and asked Ida where her white "sponsors" were. Boldly, she declared that she was a taxpayer and her children had as much right to enjoy the zoo as anyone. After they were safely on the streetcar home, she burst out laughing at her own audacity.

Lacking friends in the neighborhood, Ralph amused himself by searching for treasures in the alleys. On one of his excursions, he met Henry "Hoolie" Davis, son of a white Episcopal minister. Hoolie had rheumatic fever, which weakened his heart, so his mother homeschooled him. She welcomed Ralph as a guest.

The boys had many of the same interests. One of their projects was the construction of a radio made from copper wire wound around cardboard ice cream cylinders salvaged from a garbage can. The experience encouraged Ralph's lifelong interest in electronics, and being friends with Hoolie gave him insight into the lives of white people.

He lost contact with Hoolie when the Ellisons moved back to their old neighborhood to be closer to school and church. Ida worried about her children being isolated while she was at work. She felt the boys needed the emotional support of family and friends. Still, their frequent moves and having to live in crowded conditions with relatives made Ralph feel insecure and ashamed of their poverty.

Living in the black section of town allowed Ralph to form lasting friendships. Frank Meade, a talented young artist, lived next door. He drew caricatures of black heroes like Cowboy Bill Pickett, a famous rodeo performer, and black "buffalo" soldiers, so-called by Plains Indian tribes because their curly hair was reminiscent of the forelock of a buffalo. Ralph helped make up stories that Frank turned into comic strips.

Frank's dad, Joseph Meade, was a barber and a musician. In his backyard, under an apricot tree, he taught Frank to play trumpet and Ralph to play the brass alto horn. Soon the boys were spending more time with music than cartoons. Meade took them along to local jam sessions, and he encouraged them to listen to Alphonso Trent's band, broadcast on the radio from the Adolphus Hotel in Dallas. Because the hotel was segregated, these popular musicians had to use the back door and a freight elevator.

Another of Ralph's friends was James Edward "Jimmy" Stewart, who always wore a battered felt hat. Together, they swam in the Canadian River, hunted rabbits, and watched baseball games from a hill because they had no money for admission. Years later, as an Oklahoma civil rights leader, Stewart often traveled to New York for NAACP meetings. He always carried a package of barbecued ribs in his luggage to share with his old friend.

Ralph's part-time jobs helped him build self-confidence, and his wages contributed to the family's income.

One of his jobs was delivering packages for Randolph's Drugstore on his bicycle and working as a soda jerk at the fountain. He listened to the old men who sat on benches in front of the store as they told stories. Later, in his own writing, he used their adventures and story-telling techniques, especially exaggeration, irony, and "signifying"—making allusions to things understood by members of the black community.

He also read and sold the *Black Dispatch* newspaper. Editor and publisher Roscoe Dunjee, a "bandy-legged, hawk-nosed, brilliant, luminous man," lambasted racism, segregation, and the sorry state of school facilities for blacks in Oklahoma City. He insisted the United States Declaration of Independence, which clearly stated that all men were created equal, could not be ignored. After Dunjee discovered that blacks were forbidden to enter the Oklahoma City Carnegie Library, he threatened a lawsuit. In response, city officials opened the Paul Lawrence Dunbar Branch Library in a former pool hall. The books that the city provided there were not new, but Ralph vowed to read them all.

Although the Frederick Douglass School building was in need of repairs, its all-black faculty was well educated and maintained high standards. Its first super-intendent had been Johnson Chestnut Whittaker, a former slave once owned by Senator James Chestnut Jr. of South Carolina. Through the senator's influence, the fair-skinned youth had been admitted to the United States Military Academy. When other cadets discovered he was part African American, they harassed him physically and mentally until he was forced to leave. He came to Oklahoma, bringing to the Frederick Douglass School strict military discipline and the tradition of a well-drilled marching band.

Principal Inman Page, a former slave from Virginia, had come to Frederick Douglass after his retirement from a thirty-year career as president of Langston University in Oklahoma and Lincoln University in Missouri. His dignified, authoritarian manner and ability to speak extemporaneously awed the student body.

Years later, after Ralph Ellison became a famous writer, he was invited to speak at Brown University to honor Dr. Page, the first African American to graduate from that university. In his speech, Ellison explained the irony of being chosen to pay tribute to Dr. Page. Back in 1927, rowdy junior-high classmates had shoved Ralph into Page as they marched on stage for an assembly. Page grabbed Ralph by the back of his collar and shook him hard, shouting, "What do you think you're doing, boy? What do you think you're doing?" Then Page chased Ralph up the center aisle and out the back door while the student body roared with laughter. Thereafter Ralph had avoided Page until his senior year, when the principal presented his diploma.

Page's daughter, Zelia Page Breaux, a graduate of Lincoln University, was an accomplished musician and strict disciplinarian who administered a rigorous music program at Frederick Douglass School. She believed

Ellison's music teacher in Oklahoma City, Mrs. Zelia Page Breaux, played a large role in shaping Ellison's sense of what it meant to be an artist. (Oklahoma Historical Society)

that music was the gateway to success for black children. By developing their natural talents, she helped them achieve self-confidence. All students were required to participate in vocal music, band, and music-appreciation classes.

Mrs. Breaux directed operettas and assembly programs with multicultural themes. She taught her students Christmas carols from many lands, Scottish folk dances, Irish jigs, and how to weave the maypole. Breaux and her father provided the school with two grand pianos, a record player, and band instruments for children who could not afford them.

Wearing white shirts and pants and black ties and

caps, Breaux's high school marching band participated in holiday parades. The twenty-five young men had a repertoire that included military marches and syncopated swing marches. Ralph's favorites were Sousa's "Stars and Stripes Forever," Art Tatum's "Tiger Rag," and Rossini's "William Tell Overture." Although Breaux concentrated on traditional music at school, she hired blues and jazz performers at the Aldridge Theater, which she owned.

Black musicians toured on the Theater Owners Booking Association (TOBA) circuit and performed in dance halls, taverns, and on the vaudeville stage. Bands usually had a brass section, guitar, bass, piano, drum, and sometimes a banjo. The trumpet usually set the basic theme for instrumental improvisations and vocal solos. When they played the blues, the band accompanied the vocalist with simple chords, two- or three-part harmony.

During his high school years, Ralph played first chair trumpet and acted as student director of the Frederick Douglass band. He also played on the football team. At halftime, he ran under the grandstand, stripped off his football suit, pulled on his band uniform, and marched onto the field with the band. After their halftime performance, he changed uniforms again, just in time to line up for the kickoff.

Although he tended to resent criticism, Zelia Breaux taught Ralph that practice and self-discipline were essential to musical excellence. Through her influence, Ellison was later awarded a musical scholarship to Tuskegee Institute.

Lamonia McFarland, Ralph's English teacher, introduced him to such famous African-American writers as Phillis Wheatley, W. E. B. Du Bois, James Weldon Johnson, Countee Cullen, Claude McKay, and Langston Hughes. She told her students about the Harlem Renaissance, an artistic movement that began in the Harlem neighborhood of far-off New York City and had become the center of African-American culture.

When Ralph and his friends learned about the Harlem Renaissance, they decided to become Renaissance men themselves. Seven of them solemnly swore to learn about the world beyond Oklahoma City and to excel as "universal men" in government, sports, music, art, and literature. Even though Ralph and his friends imagined themselves as successful men of the world, they were fully aware of the obstacles of racial discrimination they would face if they ventured beyond their segregated neighborhood in Oklahoma City.

There was another question facing young African Americans, specifically about their identity, as they considered what kind of men and women they wanted to be. Growing up black in Oklahoma in the early twentieth century might not have been as dangerous as it was in the Deep South, but it was still challenging. The heritage of slavery and the ever-present racism made it difficult for them to love their country. But Mrs. McFarland told her students to think of themselves as Americans. "I am not an African since I am many generations removed from my African-born ancestry. [I

was] born in America of a mixed blood parentage," she said. "I am an American citizen." Ralph never forgot her emphasis on American citizenship, which became a basic element in his identity. For this reason, he preferred to use the term Negro American instead of African American. As an adult, Ralph attributed his "cold, Oklahoma Negro eye," meaning his practical, realistic attitude about life, to his experiences in his Deep Deuce neighborhood.

Opposite: *This painting by Edward Burra depicts a street scene in Harlem during the height of the Harlem Renaissance.* (Courtesy of the Granger Collection.)

TWO
JAZZ IN
DEEP DEUCE

During Ralph's teens, Ida Ellison kept a close eye on her older son. She did not want him hanging around juke joints and pool halls. She hoped he would someday achieve fame as a classical musician or as an intellectual. He was teased by other boys, who called him a mama's boy. Ida apparently did not realize that while he was sweeping the floor and shining shoes in "Fat" Hallie Richardson's barber shop, Ralph was hearing gossip and off-color jokes. Men gambled and drank bootleg whiskey in the back room.

Although Ralph was too young to enter Slaughter's Dance Hall, he could hear the jazzmen playing "free-wheeling, caterwauling, gutbucket stomp music" on Saturday nights and into Sunday mornings. They played lively and syncopated swing until midnight. Then they played the blues, a word derived from the phrase "blue devils," meaning a melancholy mood. To Ralph, their jazz and blues expressed loneliness and tragedy, but it also expressed their optimism and love of life.

The 1920s saw an increase in the popularity of jazz and blues, which were rooted in a combination of Western music and the spirituals and work songs traced to Africa and the slave experience. Blues and the more complex jazz expressed the hopes and dreams of a long-suffering people. Some listeners, both black and white, were offended by the earthy sound and themes of the music. Over the decades of the twentieth century, however, this authentic American art form came to represent the deepest despair and hopes of millions of people of all races.

Towns like Oklahoma City that allowed jazz bands and dancing were called "dancing towns." Some Midwestern cities and towns had laws forbidding this music on the grounds that the moves of jazz (or stomp) dancing were immoral. Popular jazz bands traveled a circuit between Kansas City, Oklahoma City, New Orleans, Memphis, and St. Louis. Eventually, the best bands headed east to Chicago and Harlem.

Members of one band, the Oklahoma City Blue Devils, had a blue imp embroidered on the pockets of their jackets. Ralph admired their instrumental techniques. Self-disciplined and independent, their lives dedicated to music, they represented success and escape from poverty. He liked their clothes and the way they walked.

He began to wave his hair with pomade and hot rags. His idols were Walter "Big 'Un" Page and his brother, Oran "Hot Lips" Page, original members of the Blue Devils. A huge man, Walter played tuba, string bass, and baritone saxophone, and Oran played trumpet.

During a set of this "blues-driven stomp music," the lead trumpet player would establish a basic theme, and then each of the other musicians, in turn, would "cut in" and challenge the previous performer with variations on this theme. At jam sessions, jazzmen competed in "cutting" contests to determine which musicians could sit in with the band.

Their fans compared these jam sessions to a religious revival, with "Reverend" Jimmy Rushing singing in his high, clear tenor voice, Hot Lips Page signifying and encouraging him, and Big 'Un tapping his foot and slapping his belly (playing bass). One of Rushing's first recordings was "Blue Devil Blues." Eventually, several members of the Blue Devils joined Bennie Moten's band in Kansas City with William "Count" Basie at piano and Lester "Pres" Young on saxophone.

Singer Jimmy Rushing had worked at his dad's lunch counter in Oklahoma City before he joined the Blue Devils. In 1958, Ellison wrote "Remembering Jimmy," for *Saturday Review.* He recalled Rushing's tenor voice, which could be heard over clanging freight trains and a twelve-piece band in Slaughter's dance hall. Rushing's voice was "like a blue flame in the dark . . . soaring high above the trumpets and trombones . . . [calling out]

This photograph shows big-band legend Count Basie, once a member of the Oklahoma City Blue Devils, on piano during a jam session. (Courtesy of Getty Images.)

'Baaaaay-bay! Tell me what's the matter now.'"

Rushing, whose squat, broad body inspired the song "Mr. Five-by-Five," made blues and jazz dancing inseparable. Despite his size, he was a graceful dancer who glided around the floor, alone or with a partner, as he sang. One of his favorite dance steps was called "falling off the log." Later, Rushing sang with Count Basie's orchestra.

Count Basie accompanied singers in vaudeville shows before he joined the Blue Devils and, later, Bennie Moten's Kansas City Orchestra. His syncopated, precise style of playing the piano set the tone of modern jazz.

He adopted the title "Count" to compete with another famous musician, Duke Ellington. Count Basie's most popular numbers were "One O'Clock Jump" and "Jumpin' at the Woodside."

Other famous blues and jazz artists played gigs at Ruby's Grill, Slaughter's Dance Hall, and the Aldridge Theater, where a local pit orchestra accompanied performers like Bessie Smith, "Empress of the Blues." When the famed Louis "Satchmo" Armstrong came to Oklahoma City to play a dance at Slaughter's, unescorted white women attended even though it was against the segregation laws.

Ralph heard Duke Ellington's band at Slaughter's with Ethel Waters as featured vocalist. Waters was billed as "Sweet Mama Stringbean." She went on to star on Broadway in Irving Berlin's *As Thousands Cheer* and in other revues and award-winning films. Later, she toured with Billy Graham's ministry as a gospel singer.

The Christian brothers, talented local musicians, attended Frederick Douglass School with Ralph. They could not afford guitars, so they constructed amazingly resonant instruments from cigar boxes. Charlie, Clarence, and Edward often walked the residential streets of Oklahoma City with their blind father, serenading wealthy residents for money.

Edward Christian became the leader of the Jolly Jugglers, a local jazz band that Ralph played with because he was good at sight-reading music. Charlie Christian later became the first person to play an electric

Duke Ellington accompanies his band on piano during a concert. (Library of Congress)

guitar in jazz and helped to break the color barrier by joining the previously all-white Benny Goodman Sextet. As a youth, he had refused to play in the Frederick Douglass School band because he liked to improvise instead of sticking to the written music, and he did not like to march.

Hoping to improve his skills on trumpet, young Ellison took private lessons from Ludwig Hebestreit, the music director at all-white Classen Senior High. The professor, who also played trumpet with the Oklahoma Symphony Orchestra, showed Ralph how to arrange music for an orchestra and encouraged him to dream of composing a jazz symphony someday. Ralph mowed Hebestreit's lawn to pay for his lessons. He had the best of both worlds—formal classical instruction with Zeila Breaux and Hebestreit, then blues and jazz in his Deep Deuce neighborhood.

In 1931, during his senior year at Frederick Douglass, Ralph decided to expand his interests. In addition to playing football and in the band, he joined the debate team and portrayed a villain in one of Breaux's operettas. The marching band toured towns in Oklahoma, Kansas, and Colorado. As a result of these extracurricular activities, Ralph neglected his studies and failed to graduate until 1932.

In the meantime, he began thinking about scholarship applications to college, maybe Langston, Fisk, or Howard—all segregated schools. Ellison needed money for tuition, so he applied for a job at a used-car lot. At the interview, the white owner sat in a lawn chair under a tree and asked Ralph to sit across from him on a metal box. It was a very hot day, but the man questioned Ellison at length about his family and school activities. Suddenly, Ellison leaped high in the air. The man had slyly given him a "hot seat," sending an electrical shock through the metal box. He thought his prank was hilarious, but Ellison felt humiliated and angry.

Ellison worked as a waiter at a country club, riding the streetcar to work. Later, he worked as a stocker and elevator operator at Lewisohns, a large department store. In the men's department, he learned about fabrics and fashion. He developed an appreciation for well-cut, fashionable clothes that lasted the rest of his life.

The job at Lewisohns kept him on edge because white women rode the elevator. Ellison had never forgotten the riot in Tulsa that was sparked by an allegation that a black man had groped a white woman in an elevator. In self-defense, Ellison adopted a cool persona when confronted by Jim Crow restrictions. He listened for the tone of a person's voice. If white racists tried to make him feel powerless and afraid, he followed his mother's example of silent contempt and private laughter at their bigotry. He avoided confrontation to maintain his self-respect.

In the fall, he attended an interview at Oklahoma's Langston Agricultural and Mechanical College, an all-black school named for poet Langston Hughes's great uncle. Although Zelia Breaux had recommended Ellison, he was denied a music scholarship because the school's forty-piece marching band did not need another trumpet player. He had not saved enough money to pay his own tuition, so he continued working at Lewisohns, where he had no hope of advancement.

During the holiday season of 1932, Ellison heard a performance of the one-hundred-member Tuskegee Institute choir broadcast from the grand opening of Radio City Music Hall in New York City. Impressed by the choir's repertoire and musical perfection, Ralph Ellison sent for a catalogue and asked Mrs. Breaux to help him gain admission to Tuskegee Institute in Alabama.

Three
TUSKEGEE
INSTITUTE

Located in Macon County, Alabama, Tuskegee Institute was founded in 1881 by Booker T. Washington for the purpose of educating freed slaves. Washington believed that vocational training for black students would improve their economic and social status. He advocated gradual, nonviolent progress toward attaining civil rights and argued that racial segregation actually helped preserve African-American culture. In speeches, he compared American citizenship to a hand, with each racial group represented by a separate but essential finger.

Remembered fondly as the founder, Washington was a successful fund-raiser, receiving many donations from wealthy white patrons and legislators who viewed his approach to race relations as nonthreatening. He was

Influential scholar and educator Booker T. Washington sits at his desk at the Tuskegee Institute in 1900.

able to expand Tuskegee Institute from one room to a campus of redbrick buildings on 2,500 beautifully land-scaped acres. The school became famous for George Washington Carver's agricultural research and its teacher-education and music programs.

In contrast to Washington's approach, Harvard gradu-ate W. E. B. Du Bois, a professor at Atlanta University, advocated an intensive liberal arts education for elite black students. He insisted this "talented tenth" would lead the masses to a better life. In his book *The Souls of Black Folk* (1903), he argued that Washington's policy of accommodation to white people's expectations would

condemn African Americans to remain the servant class of society.

In 1909, Du Bois helped organize the National Association for the Advancement of Colored People (NAACP). He became editor of its magazine, *The Crisis,* for which he wrote powerful editorials about segregation laws and other racial injustices. After World War I, he demanded recognition and support for black veterans who had fought overseas but returned home to joblessness, poverty, and Jim Crow laws.

During his travels for the NAACP, Du Bois became interested in descendants of transplanted Africans around the world. He supported the International Communist Party because he believed communism would benefit people of color. During the 1950s, when Russia became a political and military enemy of the United States, Du Bois was accused of writing subversive Communist propaganda and being the unregistered agent of a foreign power. Although he was acquitted of the charge of treason, he exiled himself to Ghana, Africa, becoming a citizen of that country and staying until his death in 1963.

Du Bois's intellectual approach was itself different from that of Marcus Garvey, whose Universal Negro Improvement Association (UNIA) promised freedom, justice, and equality for all descendants of Africans. In 1920, Garvey solicited funds to purchase ships, on which he planned to transport black Americans to Africa, which he said was the only place they could ever be truly free.

Marcus Garvey was well known for his controversial and radical ideas regarding the "back to Africa" movement. (Library of Congress)

Many of the buildings on the Tuskegee campus were built by students at the university. In addition to agricultural and domestic trades, building was considered a valuable and dignified skill that would bring pride and competence to members of the African-American community. (Library of Congress)

Garvey used emotional appeals—street-corner speeches, pep rallies, bands, uniforms, and colorful flags—to recruit supporters and money for his "back to Africa" movement. However, the UNIA's lack of organization and financial mismanagement doomed the venture. Garvey was eventually jailed for fraud and deported to Jamaica, his birthplace.

In 1933, when young Ralph Ellison applied for acceptance as a freshman at Tuskegee Institute, he was unaware of Washington's ideas about segregation and accommodation, Du Bois's interest in communism, or Garvey's Afrocentrism. Insulated by the values and culture of the Oklahoma community in which he was raised, Ellison had his own ideas about how to cope with racism. He assumed an impassive mask and avoided confrontation. His focus was on earning a degree in music and becoming a composer.

Dr. William Levi Dawson, head of the music department at Tuskegee, received Zelia Breaux's recommendation. She wrote that Ellison was "industrious and a very splendid scholar." He agreed to interview Ellison and to give him an audition in July.

Ellison's plan had been to work all summer and save his money for train fare to Alabama, arriving just in time for school to start. He owed payments on a new Conn cornet, and he wanted to buy new clothes. But the chance for a tryout date changed his plan. He had to move faster. Without money for a train or bus ticket, Ellison, in desperation, turned to an acquaintance who was an accomplished freight-train jumper. Charlie was an African-American jockey who could pass for white, an asset that allowed him more freedom in the South. He accompanied Ellison part of the way to Alabama and gave him advice about how to survive in a "hobo jungle."

First, Charlie taught Ellison how to jump on board a moving boxcar and how to read the car's destination. Then he warned him about railroad "bulls," policemen who bumped riders off trains with clubs or arrested them and made them work on a chain gang. He told Ellison how to secure the basic necessities of food and water while traveling and how to use the bathroom facilities in segregated Southern towns. He also warned him about racist hoboes, thieves, and sexual predators. For protection, Ellison carried a switchblade knife in his pocket.

Illegally riding the rails through the South was dangerous enough for a young black man, but it was made even more so by a recent case in Alabama. Nine black men had been arrested and charged with raping two white women. Though one woman later recanted and the other's story was questionable, all nine men, called the Scottsboro Boys by the press, were convicted and sentenced to either death or life in prison.

In 1932, the U.S. Supreme Court overturned their convictions on the grounds they did not have adequate legal representation. Future appeals resulted in the reduction of some sentences, but the last defendant was not paroled until 1951. The case generated national attention and sparked much outrage.

When Ellison and several other riders were forced off a train in Decatur, Alabama, he feared the worst. During the ensuing skirmish, a railroad bull hit Ellison with his stick. Expecting to be shot in the back, Ellison ran for his life and hid in a lumber warehouse. He arrived at Tuskegee Institute just in time to have his freshman picture made with a bandage on his forehead.

After the interview and audition, Dr. Dawson awarded Ellison a music scholarship and classified him as a work-study student, which meant he had to work on campus. One of his duties was shelving books in the Hollis Burke Frissell Library, a job that gave him access to many excellent volumes. Compulsory reading for freshmen included Booker T. Washington's *Up from Slavery*.

Ellison was assigned a room in Thrasher Hall that, in 1933, had no plumbing. Showers and toilets were in a separate facility. Freshmen were required to wear uniforms and to follow strict rules that kept them regimented and submissive. They had to participate in military drills and attend study hall each night.

In order to go to the shops across the street from the campus, students had to get permission from a dormitory proctor. To avoid unpleasant encounters with white people, freshmen were forbidden to enter the town. These rules annoyed Ellison.

Even though the music faculty did not approve, Ellison occasionally left the campus with a jazz combo to play dances at a nearby veteran's hospital and at Fort Benning. Travel through small southern towns was risky for young black men. Even a slight traffic violation could result in a heavy fine, harassment, or jail. Under the worst circumstances, too many ended up dead by lynching.

Ellison's talent had secured him a music scholarship at Tuskegee, but segregation laws and threats of brutality in the South frustrated him. Racial restrictions in Oklahoma were mild compared to the Jim Crow laws in Alabama.

When classes began in September, Ellison became acquainted with the music faculty. Two of his favorite teachers were Captain Drye, the band director and trumpet teacher, and Hazel Harrison, the piano teacher. Drye, a former army bandmaster, had once been Dizzy Gillespie's teacher. In the 1940s, Gillespie would become famous as one of the founders of modern bebop jazz. Drye nicknamed Ellison "Sousa" and appointed him student conductor of the band at football games.

Harrison, a classical pianist, had studied in Europe

and was a friend of the composer Sergei Prokofiev. She became Ellison's confidante and advisor, much as Zelia Breaux had been in Oklahoma City. She taught Ellison to always play his best, no matter where he was. He could never know who might be listening.

Dr. Dawson directed the famous Tuskegee choir. He also composed and arranged music for vocal and instrumental ensembles at the school. He had been first trombonist with the Chicago Symphony Orchestra. At Carnegie Hall, Leopold Stokowski had conducted Dawson's *Negro Symphony No. 1,* a work rich in African-American folk themes.

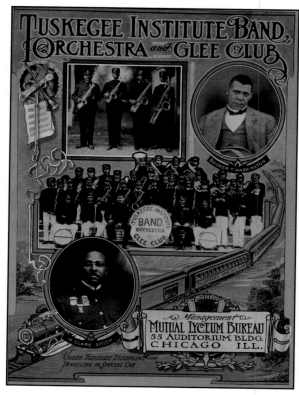

This poster promoting a concert in Chicago by the Tuskegee band, orchestra, and glee club in Chicago gives some idea of the high-profile nature of the Tuskegee music program. (Library of Congress)

Dawson demanded excellence from his students. He was a harsh critic who occasionally threw chalk or hymnals at students who did not perform as he expected. After Ellison's first solo performance, Dawson admonished him for trying to interpret the piece instead of playing it as the composer wrote it.

Drye insisted that the classical trumpet should have a brilliant, militant tone, not the muted, raspy tone of blues and jazz, which mimicked a gravely-voiced vocalist. Neither Dawson nor Drye approved of jazz, which they considered nonstandard and unrefined.

Robert Moton, Tuskegee's president, was a physically impressive and charismatic man, skilled at obtaining donations to Tuskegee from wealthy white patrons. On Founder's Day, when trustees visited the campus, the band and choir performed a concert and students marched before the dignitaries for inspection. While the formal ceremony was taking place in Logan Hall, African Americans from the surrounding area gathered outside, enjoying picnics, ball games, and dances. Ellison longed to be outdoors with them instead of sitting in the orchestra pit, compelled to listen to boring speeches.

Moton emphasized the need for faculty and students to modify their behavior to the expectations of white patrons. Ellison, an acute observer, noticed that Moton kept his hands behind his back so the white trustees would not be forced to shake his hand. He realized that Moton had both a public and a private persona and began to wonder what the real Moton was like. Ellison heard him speak twice daily in Logan Hall, at morning assembly and at vespers. Like Booker T. Washington, Moton promoted the stereotype of the "Negro as . . . cheerful and buoyant, emotional and demonstrative, keen of apprehension, ambitious, persistent, responsive to authority, and deeply religious."

Ellison wanted to debate the accuracy of this stereotype, but students were not permitted to question teachers. He considered the faculty unfriendly but reasoned that they adopted strict, authoritarian attitudes in order to model correct speech, dress, and manners for their students. In American society, especially in Alabama, these well-educated, African-American professors received no more respect from white residents than did their students.

Ellison liked his English professor, Morteza Drexel Sprague, an excellent lecturer and popular composition teacher. Sprague coached the debate team and sponsored the Ki Yi social club. In his home, members discussed art, music, and literature as they munched on cookies and drank punch.

Sprague assigned daily essays of six hundred to seven hundred words. Writing these essays helped Ellison improve his vocabulary, grammar, and spelling skills. In Sprague's British literature class, Ellison learned how to analyze the plot and characterization techniques of master writers such as Charles Dickens and Thomas Hardy. In 1964, Ellison dedicated *Shadow and Act,* a collection of essays, to Sprague. He acknowledged that although he had been consciously studying to become a musician while he was in Sprague's class, he had been learning skills that helped him become a writer.

In a sociology class, Ellison was astounded when a professor used a textbook that claimed all African Americans shared certain basic personality traits. These included a carefree, submissive disposition and a reliance on intuition and emotion rather than logic or reason. Ellison was outraged that his professor would encourage students to accept these demeaning stereotypes without discussing the possibility of individuality or racial diversity.

He knew that his grandfather Alfred Ellison, Lewis Ellison, J. D. Randolph, Johnson Chestnut Whittaker, Inman Page, and Roscoe Dunjee had not accepted life passively. They were proud, ambitious men who had lived brave, exemplary lives, even though state laws and customs had curtailed their equal rights and economic opportunities.

That summer, Ellison returned to Oklahoma City. Friends and neighbors welcomed him home, expecting to hear about his great accomplishments. But Ellison had failed to make the dean's list because he did not pass Dawson's class in solfeggio, the ability to sing do-re-mi-fa-so-la-ti-do in a specific key without using a pitch pipe.

He worked part time at Lewisohns and spent time with his friend Jimmy Stewart, but things were not the same. His brother Herbert was barely literate and still dependent upon their mother. Ida Ellison had remarried and was thinking of moving to Ohio. She had become active in the Socialist Party and was an outspoken opponent of housing segregation. Her beliefs had even led to a brief stint in jail. Publisher Roscoe Dunjee had bailed her out. The incident convinced Ellison that segregation laws in Oklahoma would never change. After that summer visit, he realized that Oklahoma City was no longer his home.

By the spring of 1936, Ellison had grown tired of his uninspiring classes at Tuskegee. He was also rethinking his commitment to a music career. A bored and unhappy junior, he enrolled in sociology, sculpture, and creative writing classes that had no direct application to his music major. He did this without permission from Dr. Dawson, who was on leave from the campus. He resumed his habit of self-education, reading novels and short stories by Ernest Hemingway, Mark Twain, Stephen Crane, and other writers he admired.

He read *The Negro History in Thirteen Plays* (1935) by Willis Richardson, a book of dramas about black heroes, including Crispus Attucks, Nat Turner, Frederick Douglass, Harriet Tubman, and Sojourner Truth. The introduction to Richardson's book was written by Carter G. Woodson, author of *The Mis-Education of the Negro*. Woodson believed that training blacks to conform to white society's expectations, instead of educating them about their own history, kept them submissive. Woodson created Negro History Week in 1927, which later became Black History Month.

Ellison also read *The Souls of Black Folk* and became

interested in W. E. B. Du Bois's theory of "double consciousness." Du Bois wrote that the conflict between a person's African identity and his American identity created a double consciousness, an identity crisis that was a particular burden for African Americans. Du Bois's provocative chapter "Of Booker T. Washington and Others" censured the Tuskegee faculty and students for submitting to an administrative hierarchy and modeling their behavior and dress on white society's standards. He claimed Washington's focus on vocational training served the political and economic needs of whites.

Ellison did not entirely agree with Du Bois. He felt no affinity for Africa, for example. His roots were in Oklahoma, even if the state and local segregation laws denied him his full constitutional rights as an American citizen. He did see himself as one of Du Bois's "talented tenth," a person with intellectual and artistic skills who could help other members of his race. But, like Washington, he was in favor of preserving black culture and avoiding riots and violence. Proud and independent, Ellison resented having to submit to any authority figure, black or white. He began formulating his own set of principles to live by.

During this critical time of reevaluation and self-education, Ellison read T. S. Eliot's long free-verse poem *The Waste Land*. Its rapid shifts of voice and scene and use of allusion and symbolism intrigued him and made him realize that literature could be revolutionary. The poem was both realistic and highly imaginative. Ellison

Modernist poet and author of
The Waste Land, *T. S. Eliot.*

pored over the poem's complicated structure. Its theme, the decay of modern Western civilization, appealed to him philosophically. Perhaps most importantly, *The Waste Land* appealed to his musical ear. It was structured like a modern symphony or a jazz concert. Eliot employed symbolism, metaphor, and evocative sounds through language. To understand the poem's allusions to ancient and modern cultures, Ellison researched classic literature and Greco-Roman myths, guided by the poem's numerous footnotes.

The Waste Land was representative of a new literary style called modernism. Ellison wondered if something like it might be written from an African-American perspective. It would have to contain a mixture of racial and cultural heritages, Biblical and folk allusions, standard English as well as street language, and jazz and blues rhythms with snatches from operas and pop tunes. Eliot's poem opened up the vast possibility of the study of literature to the newly disenchanted musician. Ellison later said that the seed of his future work had been planted when he read *The Waste Land's* famous line: "I will show you fear in a handful of dust."

When Dr. Dawson returned to Tuskegee and discovered that Ellison had not completed his curriculum requirements, he canceled Ellison's music scholarship. With no money for tuition, Ellison decided to spend the summer in New York City and earn enough money to finance his senior year.

In New York, however, Ellison discovered that jobs were scarce and wages minimal. During the summer, he barely earned enough to cover basic expenses, and certainly not enough to return to Tuskegee. His formal education was over, but intriguing new experiences awaited him.

Four

HARLEM

In 1936, Ellison rode the bus from Tuskegee to New York City. He took a room at the Harlem YMCA, working in the cafeteria to pay for it. Life was tough in the strange city, but he felt it was a great improvement over Alabama and Oklahoma City. Harlem had the largest black population of any city in the world, with more than 400,000 African-American residents. Still, it was not the same Harlem he had read and dreamed about with his friends in high school. The Harlem Renaissance had run into the reality of the Great Depression. Money was tight and jobs were scarce. Over half of the nation's black workers were unemployed. Few could indulge in such luxuries as books, journals, or theater tickets. Despite these problems, Harlem remained the center of black art and entertainment.

Langston Hughes, Harlem Renaissance poet and lifelong friend and mentor to Ellison. (Library of Congress)

Langston Hughes, one of the most famous of the Harlem Renaissance poets, was also a resident at the YMCA. He became Ellison's mentor and confidante. Although the initial excitement of the Harlem Renaissance had subsided, Hughes continued to travel and receive accolades for his books, poetry, plays, musical librettos, and newspaper column. His essay "The Negro Artist and the Racial Mountain" asserted that Negro artists create their work from a unique and important perspective. Hughes argued that writers who imitated the style and tone of white British and American writers showed a lack of pride in African-American culture.

Although he was not a member of the Communist political party, Hughes was a sympathizer, a "fellow traveler" with the party's goals. He encouraged Ellison's interest in Marxism and loaned him books, including Andre Malraux's *Man's Fate,* a novel set in China in 1927 during a Communist-inspired rebellion.

Hughes introduced Ellison to other notables in the arts and academia. Alain Locke was a literary critic and professor at Howard University, Edna St. Vincent Millay was famous for her lyrical poems of protest, and artist Richmond Barthe taught Ellison sculpture for a few months. Ellison also met bandleader Duke Ellington, one of his favorite musicians. Hughes gave Ellison practical advice: "Allow them to pay for your meals."

Hughes took Ellison to a performance of a play based on Erskine Caldwell's novel *Tobacco Road,* a satire about white Southern sharecroppers who maintain they are socially superior to their more prosperous and morally upright black neighbors. Ellison laughed so loudly at the irony that the actors momentarily stopped the performance.

In his free time, Ellison toured the city by subway, bus, and ferry. Harlem teemed with workers, shoppers, vagrants, and foreigners, young and old, all living in close proximity in old brownstone buildings. Odors, voices, and snatches of music assailed his senses. Here, he saw no evidence of accommodation to white standards. On street corners, preachers urged salvation and politicians advocated better housing, less crime, and urban renewal. Black nationalists denounced racial integration.

Ellison knew how to cope with racial limitations in the segregated South but was unsure how to behave in New York City. Blacks did not have to sit in the back of a subway car, and men did not give up their seats to women. He observed a white woman rudely shove a black man aside and sit in his seat. Then the man sat on her lap but leaped up when she jabbed him with a finger. Ellison expected a riot to follow, but everyone just laughed. He never grew accustomed to standing in the aisle of a subway or bus with white people packed tightly around him.

Greenwich Village, home to artists and entertainers, became one of Ellison's favorite places to visit. He loved the bookstores and the Automat cafeterias, where friends sat at tables and discussed art and current events. Soon he felt free to enter museums and other public buildings, but he discovered that some movie theaters and certain restaurants did not welcome blacks. Although no "whites only" signs were posted, a waiter gave him a subtle hint by salting his food so much it was inedible. He quickly learned to say no to scam artists and predators. In general, people on the street did not make eye contact with him. Sometimes, he felt as if he were invisible.

Ellison's job at the YMCA paid for his room and board, but he needed more money in order to return to Tuskegee, which he was still planning to do. Briefly, he

This street scene of an outdoor art exhibit in Greenwich Village gives a taste of the stimulating, creative atmosphere to which Ellison was attracted. (Courtesy of the Granger Collection.)

worked from nine to five as a temporary receptionist and file clerk for psychiatrist Harry Stack Sullivan. Then he took a job as a laborer in a paint factory. By the end of summer, he realized a return to Tuskegee was impossible. To his surprise, he felt a sense of relief. He was now free to pursue new challenges in New York City.

When he told Langston Hughes of his ambition to become a writer, Hughes loaned him a typewriter and introduced him to Richard Wright, city editor of the Communist-supported *Daily Worker* newspaper and editor of *New Challenge* magazine. Wright encouraged Ellison's new interest in Marxism as the cure for racism in America. During discussions on politics and literature, Ellison deferred to Wright as the expert, even though he had opinions, too. Their backgrounds were similar. Both had come from dysfunctional families, handicapped by poverty.

They became close friends, even though Wright was a sloppy dresser who knew little about jazz and could not dance, activities that were important to Ellison. Wright's intense concentration as he labored over his typewriter at the *Daily Worker* impressed Ellison. Later, he observed Wright's impatience with office personnel and his mistrust of other associates. He also observed that Wright could not bear to be corrected.

Wright had not graduated from high school in his home state of Mississippi, yet he had become a successful journalist in Chicago. His essay "Blueprint for Negro Writing" urged black artists to exhibit pride and self-discipline and not to be submissive to white editors. He had encouraged prizewinning poet Gwendolyn Brooks to use realism in her portrayal of scenes from her Chicago neighborhood.

Wright wrote powerful editorials and was an authority on the history and ideology of communism. During the Depression, the Communist Party USA (CPUSA) actively recruited African Americans. Jobless and im-

Writer and critic Richard Wright.
(Library of Congress)

poverished, some blacks were attracted to communism because it promised to eliminate the class system and give workers a share of the nation's wealth. It also promised freedom of expression to artists and intellectuals.

Theoretically, under communism a central government would own and administer all property and industry. Workers would receive a fair share of the wealth and goods produced by the economy. The slogan, "From each according to his ability, to each according to his need," seemed to guarantee equality regardless of color. Wright challenged party leadership for failure to live up to these promises and address the problems of African Americans.

He asked Ellison to critique a collection of short stories, later published as *Uncle Tom's Children.* Then he assigned Ellison the task of writing book reviews by contemporary authors. He showed Ellison how to tighten his writing and encouraged him to write a short story for *New Challenge* magazine. Ellison wrote "Hymie's Bull," a fictionalized account of his experience in the Alabama freight yard when the railroad bull beat him with a black jack. The magazine folded, and the story remained unpublished until 1996.

To sharpen his skills at writing fiction, Ellison analyzed and copied the style of other writers, including Ernest Hemingway and Russian Fyodor Dostoyevsky. He was particularly impressed with Dostoyevsky's *Notes from Underground,* in which the narrator hides in a cellar to escape the chaos of revolution in Russia. Using a stream-of-consciousness style, the narrator affirms his existence and free will to make choices about his future life.

Sometimes Ellison played his trumpet to get in the mood to write. He compared practicing scales, developing a tone, and controlling pitch to practicing styles of writing, developing an emotional tone, and selecting his words carefully. Using the discipline he had applied to music, he began to develop his own voice and style. Later, when he was asked how he became a writer, he laughed and said modestly, "I blundered into it."

Ellison and Wright attended the second League of American Writers Congress and heard their hero Ernest

Hemingway speak about the civil war in Spain. Hemingway was recruiting volunteers for the Abraham Lincoln Brigade to go to Spain to fight the fascist forces of General Francisco Franco, whose allies were Adolf Hitler of Germany and Benito Mussolini of Italy. Later, Ellison read another book by Malraux, *Man's Hope,* about the tragedies fascists inflicted on Spanish peasants during the civil war.

He attended a lecture at the New School for Social Research in which Kenneth Burke, a famous intellectual, explained Hitler's use of anti-Semitic propaganda to accomplish economic and social reforms in Germany. Ellison saw similarities between the scapegoat tactics used by Nazis to blame Jews for Europe's economic problems and the tactics used by white racists against African Americans in his own country.

Ellison enjoyed attending meetings of a political group, the Popular Front, which required no credentials, social status, or racial identification. Communist sponsors promoted this democratic coalition to attract new members. Members had fun "partying, boogying, and boozing." Some enjoyed interracial romances, a taboo in the South.

In 1937, Ellison received word his mother was critically ill. After moving to Dayton, Ohio, Ida had fallen and broken her hip, which had been weakened by tuberculosis of the bone. She died on October 16. In a letter to Richard Wright, he described her death as a painful emotional experience, "the end of [my] childhood."

Although relatives in Ohio were sympathetic, they were unable to offer any financial support. Without money to return to New York, Ellison turned to hunting rabbits and quail and searching abandoned farmsteads for windfalls from pear trees and nuts to supplement his food supply. For a time, Ellison and his brother Herbert stayed with an elderly great-aunt. She told them about their maternal grandfather, Polk Milsap, a slave who had guarded his master's money throughout the Civil War, then fled with it to Canada.

In the process of settling Ida's medical and burial expenses, Ellison met William O. Stokes, an attorney, who allowed him to sleep in his office and to use the bathroom facilities down the hall. At night, Ellison used Stokes's typewriter and wrote short stories on the back of the lawyer's discarded letterhead stationary.

Five

THE
APPRENTICE

I n the spring of 1938, Ellison left Herbert behind in Dayton and returned to New York. Herbert had depended on Ralph to watch out for him when they were young and would have been content with continuing that type of relationship. Although he found it difficult to admit, Ellison was not willing to give up his ambitions to care for his brother. Herbert stayed behind with family; Ralph moved on.

Back in New York, Ellison was jobless and broke again. Richard Wright recommended him to the Federal Writers' Project of New York City (NYWP), which was supported by the Works Project Administration (WPA), part of President Franklin Roosevelt's New Deal program to end the Depression. His salary was twenty-five dollars a week.

Journalist Roi Ottley administered the NYWP. Ellison observed that Ottley's major interest was women, not the NYWP. While some looked upon the project as easy money, Ellison welcomed it as his apprenticeship in journalism. On assignment, he explored the history of African Americans in New York City, dating back to the 1600s. He researched and wrote a series of articles about race riots in the United States, including the Tulsa riot of 1921.

Ellison also wrote special reports about important black leaders, including Max Yeargan, founder of the YMCAs in South Africa, and James Weldon Johnson, an administrator of the NAACP. Johnson had written *The Autobiography of an Ex-Coloured Man* (1912), *God's Trombones: Seven Negro Sermons in Verse*

James Weldon Johnson — novelist, poet, activist, and executive secretary of the NAACP from 1920 to 1931. (Library of Congress)

These documents are an example of some of the forms Ellison filled out during his interviews while working for the Federal Writers' Project of New York City. (Library of Congress)

Forms to be Filled out for Each Interview   FOLKLORE

****

FORM A   NEW YORK

Circumstances of Interview

STATE   **New York**

NAME OF WORKER   **Ralph Ellison**

ADDRESS   **470 West 150 Street**

DATE   **May 10, 1939**

SUBJECT   **Harlem**

1. Date and time of interview
   April 30, 1939   8:00 P.M.

2. Place of interview
   Eddie's Bar, St. Nicholas Avenue near 147 Street

3. Name and address of informant

4. Name and address of person, if any, who put you in touch with informant.
   Anonymous

5. Name and address of person, if any, accompanying you

6. Description of room, house, surroundings, etc.
   Modernistic barroom, green walls, marine designs, Red imitation leather upholstery. Mirrors. Nickle phonograph in rear half of room where food is served. Bronze metal work, framed. Waiter and waitress, the former in black uniform, the latter in green. All of this in good taste.

Text of Interview   (Unedited)

STATE   **New York**

NAME OF WORKER   **Ralph Ellison**

ADDRESS   **470 West 150 Street**

DATE   **May 10, 1939**

SUBJECT   **Harlem -- Ahm In New York**

       Ahm in New York, but New York aint in me. You understand? Ahm in New York, but New York aint in me. What do I mean? Listen. Im from Jacksonville Florida. Been in New York twenty-five years. Im a New Yorker! But Im in New York an New York aint in me. Yuh understand? Naw, naw, yuh dont get me. Whut do they do; take Lenox Avenue. Take Seventh Avenue; take Sugar Hill! Pimps. Numbers. Cheating these poor people outa whut they got. Shooting, cutting, backbiting, all them things. Yuh see? Yuh see whut Ah mean? I'M in New York, but New York aint in me! Dont laugh, dont laugh. Ahm laughing but Ah dont mean it; it aint funny. Yuh see. Im on Sugar Hill, but Sugar Hill aint on me.

       Ah come here twenty-five years ago. Bright lights, Pretty women. More space to move around. S'on, if Ah had-a got New York in me Ahd a-been dead a long time ago. What happened the other night. Yuh heard about the shooting up here in the hill. Take that boy. Ah knowed im! Anybody been around this hill knows im, n they know he went fo a bad man. Whatd he do? Now mind yuh now , His brothers a big-shot. Makes plenty money. Got a big car an a fine office. But

(1927), and the anthem "Lift Every Voice and Sing."

Another of Ellison's projects for the NYWP was researching and collecting children's stories, games, rhymes, and folk tales, such as the one about "Sweet the Monkey," who can make himself invisible. It reminded him of playing games and chanting rhymes on the playground at the Frederick Douglass School in Oklahoma City. The project published his collection of folk rhymes, "Chase the White Horse," in the *Journal of the American Folklore Society.*

When Langston Hughes returned to Harlem, Ellison told him about Ida's death and confessed his shame at his family's poverty. When he showed Hughes a portfolio of stories he had written, Hughes was encouraging.

Ellison's friendship with Richard Wright had become an important part of his education in literature. Although Wright assumed the role of teacher, Ellison read and critiqued Wright's short story collection, *Uncle Tom's Children,* published in 1938. He read Wright's novel, *Native Son,* page by page as it was being written and made suggestions. They discussed the use of dialect to reflect regional speech and the stream-of-consciousness technique, in which an author attempts to capture how thoughts course through a character's mind. Inspired, Ellison started writing *Slick,* his own protest novel, about an unemployed and frustrated black laborer.

While an employee of the NYWP, Ellison observed things that made him skeptical of the Communist Party's interest in African Americans. The slogan "Black and White, Unite and Fight!" seemed hypocritical when he learned that most labor unions excluded black workers, or used the same onerous membership requirements, like difficult literacy tests, that whites in the South used to keep blacks from voting. It was also obvious that Communist leaders were more interested in promoting international communism than in securing jobs for unemployed black Americans.

Ellison also observed that some African-American party leaders displayed domineering attitudes toward their black subordinates but were submissive to white leaders who exhibited attitudes of "condescension, patronage, mockery, and duplicity." Their relationships reminded him of the white philanthropists and black administrators at Tuskegee. Ellison disliked being sub-missive toward anyone. But as he had done at Tuskegee, he kept his thoughts to himself.

Ellison decided to move to a room in Greenwich Village, where he met Romare Bearden, an artist who worked for the welfare department. Together, they explored art galleries and museums, danced at the Savoy Ballroom, and laughed at Buck and Bubbles' act at the Apollo Theater. Bearden told stories of his experiences growing up in Harlem, and Ellison shared his memories of Oklahoma. Ellison liked to watch "Romie" paint abstract pictures of Negro workers in urban and rural environments while they discussed the connection between art, music, and literature.

This colorful Romare Bearden collage, entitled Melon Season, *gives a sense of both the folksiness and experimental nature of his art.* (Courtesy of Art Resource, (c) Romare Bearden Foundation / Licensed by VAGA, New York, NY.)

They decided a combination of the tragic and the comic would best portray African-American life in all genres of art. "Blues-toned laughter" had sustained black musicians through blues and jazz. Why not a fiction style modeled on blues and jazz? Ellison had not forgotten T. S. Eliot's *The Waste Land,* with its tragic themes embedded in lines of poetry that resembled jazz.

Bearden began creating unique collages with found materials, odds and ends that appealed to him. Ellison suggested he call his work visual jazz. Bright colors replaced the trumpet's blare. Rectangles and vertical lines were the drumbeats, and found materials became unique interpretations of a basic theme and captured the improvisational quality of the best jazz solos. Ellison saw Bearden's art as a metaphor for America, "a collage of a nation, a culture made out of improvisations." He applauded the way Bearden's art revealed complex experiences, "the mystery which gets left out of history." Ellison and Bearden remained lifelong friends.

About this time, Ellison met Rose Poindexter, a dancer and actress in the cast of Langston Hughes's play *Don't You Want to Be Free?,* at the Harlem Suitcase Theater. Later, she appeared in the revue *Saturday Night in Harlem,* which included a hilarious parody of *Gone With the Wind.* They began dating, and she and Ralph were married by a justice of the peace in New Haven, Connecticut, on September 17, 1938. But her busy career and his work schedule placed a strain on the marriage. They separated and finally divorced in 1945.

In 1938, Ellison began working part time as a reviewer for *New Masses,* a publication associated with the Communist Party. He was surprised at the magazine's editorial policies, which blacklisted the long-dead Russian novelist Fyodor Dostoyevsky on the grounds he was an anti-Semite and American writer Henry James, also dead, as a snob. They were two of Ellison's favorite authors. Later, *New Masses* lifted its strict political guidelines in order to better compete with the *Partisan Review,* an influential, progressive but anti-Communist journal of criticism and fiction that emphasized intellectual and artistic freedom.

During the 1939 American Writer's Conference, Ellison shared his short stories with the poet Margaret Walker, a friend of Richard Wright's. She urged Ellison to write more about Riley and Buster, eleven-year-old boys whose adventures were modeled after those of Ellison and his boyhood friend Frank Meade. The stories contained songs and rhymes that Ellison had learned in childhood. He sold a few, and they were republished after Ellison's death.

At the same conference, Ellison met Sanora Babb, a white writer from California. They began a love affair that was complicated not only by a continent's distance between them but also by taboos of segregation. When she came to visit, Ellison had to sneak up stairways to her hotel room because New York hotels were racially segregated. Though Ellison would eventually become critical of black men who married white women, as though their ability to do so was a sign of their success, he was honest about his love for Babb. They would remain close for years.

In 1939, as Europe headed toward the outbreak of World War II, political tensions increased in the United States. During the long economic depression of the 1930s, when the capitalist system seemed to be in decline, the Communist Party had attracted members and gained influence in intellectual circles. Some political leaders from the Democratic and Republican parties saw this influence as a threat; others seized upon it as a political issue that could serve their personal ambitions. One congressional committee, the House Committee on Un-American Activities, led by southern Democrat and segregationist Martin Dies, made headlines with its announced intention to root out all Communist influence. Dies was also opposed to most of President Roosevelt's New Deal programs. He had the committee investigate the NYWP and accused it of publishing subversive propaganda. Many of Ellison's coworkers were fired, but he remained on staff. In 1940, the federal government withdrew its support from the NYWP. By this time, Ellison had begun writing full time for *New Masses*.

Events in Europe made officials in the United States wary of international communism. In 1939, only weeks before German troops invaded Poland and began World War II, Joseph Stalin, dictator of the Union of Soviet Socialist Republics (USSR), signed a nonaggression

WONDER HOW LONG THE HONEYMOON WILL LAST?

This American cartoon questions the strange alliance between Hitler and Stalin at the beginning of World War II. (Library of Congress)

pact with Adolf Hitler. Hitler had risen to power by attacking Soviet communism, and this agreement indicated that Stalin was more concerned about his own political future and that of the Soviet Union than he was about the cause of international communism. Strategically, the agreement freed Hitler from worrying about an attack from the Soviet Union while he destroyed the small Polish army and then turned his attention to France and Great Britain in the west. Eventually, in August of 1941, Hitler broke the treaty and invaded the Soviet Union.

The Stalin-Hitler pact, as it came to be called, permanently damaged the Communist cause in the United States. Many American Communists withdrew from the party. Others viewed Stalin's pact as a pragmatic move to keep Communist Russia out of war. At the time, Americans were unaware of the Nazi's genocidal extermination of European Jews and of Stalin's extermination of millions of Russians who opposed his totalitarian rule.

Richard Wright's novel *Native Son* sold 200,000 copies and made him a celebrity. It received rave reviews until a diverse group of Communist intellectuals, black nationalists, and conservatives began to complain that the novel did not offer solutions to racist degradation. Ellison wrote to Wright, who was in Mexico, that "no one here seems aware of how really nationalistic [*Native Son*] happens to be. It is NEGRO American lit."

In spite of Ellison's loyalty to Wright, their friendship began to fade. Wright's fame had attracted important new friends. He was also becoming difficult to be around. Ellison generously attributed Wright's irascible temper and mood swings to hard work on his photo-history, *Twelve Million Black Voices*. He had also recently divorced his wife, Dheema. However, he had not told Ellison of his secret marriage to another white woman, Ellen Poplar.

When he asked Wright to critique *Slick,* his unfinished novel, Wright read it and replied sarcastically, "That's my stuff!" He accused Ellison of copying his style and cheating him over a debt of Dheema's. Ellison was offended. He later abandoned *Slick* and never asked Wright to critique his work again.

Ellison was beginning to gain recognition as a book reviewer at *New Masses*. He bought his own typewriter and returned the one Langston Hughes had loaned him. The two men seldom saw each other. Ellison was busy developing his career, and Hughes was frequently on speaking tours.

Ellison began spending more time with people like Kenneth Burke, theorist and editor of the Federal Writers' Project, and Stanley Hyman, critic at the *New Yorker* magazine. They knew how to organize words to make arguments and how to devise metaphors and strategies to create literary art in nonfiction. They convinced him friendship between blacks and whites was possible.

Ellison was reading widely as well as learning from his new friends. He began to focus on the way authors present historical, political, and economic settings. He thought these forces should determine characterization and plot in a novel. He sometimes analyzed characterization from a psychological point of view. His reviews usually had a similar structure. Each gave an overview and a plot summary, discussed a particularly interesting element, and then finished with comments.

In 1940, Ellison traveled to Washington, D.C., to attend the third National Negro Congress. He described what happened in "A Congress Jim Crow Didn't Attend" for *New Masses*. Washington was a segregated city, so facilities in hotels were not available for the delegates. They camped in tents near the Washington Monument. Speakers discussed economic issues, the need for civil rights, New Deal social-welfare programs, and argued over America's entry in the European war that had begun in September 1939. One of the speakers, A. Philip Randolph, founding president of the Brotherhood of Sleeping Car Porters and editor of the *Messenger,* asked the audience to reject Communist-controlled unions. Communists in the audience heckled him, but Randolph insisted that the Communist unions were not representing black workers. Although the United States had not yet declared war, factories were building weapons and supplies and shipping them overseas, which had created thousands of new jobs in the still-weak economy. How-

Labor and civil rights organizer A. Philip Randolph. (Library of Congress)

ever, few African Americans had been given any of these jobs. Randolph's influence as a labor and civil rights leader was growing. Later, after he threatened to organize a march on Washington in protest, President Roosevelt hastily issued an executive order barring racial discrimination in all federal projects involving war industries.

But at the conference, Ellison thought Randolph had betrayed the Communists who sponsored the meeting. Later, when he realized Randolph had demanded civil rights for African Americans and got immediate results without any help from the Communist party, Ellison rethought his criticism of Randolph, whose audacity made him an effective leader in the civil rights movement as it escalated during and after the war.

Ellison began to question the effectiveness of communism in solving the problem of racism in America. Disappointed at the party's failure to strongly support civil rights for African Americans, he drifted further away. His interest was always more in the arts and in capturing the experiences of American blacks. His fundamental impulse toward life was not political but artistic. His rebellious impulses, and genuine anger and concern about the oppression of African Americans, began to find expression in his writing as he became a more confident writer.

Six

A Changing World, A Changing Life

I n June 1941, Ellison attended an executive committee meeting of the League of American Writers to discuss ways to publicize worldwide poverty. He suggested that blues lyrics were the perfect art form for expressing social tragedies related to poverty. White committee members said his ideas were too superficial. Their disdain infuriated him.

His impatience with Communists, apathetic academics, intellectuals, and Harlem Renaissance anachronisms spilled over in "Stormy Weather," his negative review of Langston Hughes's autobiography, *The Big Sea*. Ellison praised Hughes's wonderful sensory images and interesting anecdotes but felt his old friend had glossed over his harsh and impoverished youth and his struggle to succeed as a writer. Ellison encouraged other black writers to disclose the diversity of African-American experiences.

In the summer of 1941, as Europe was being overrun by German troops and Hitler was finalizing his secret plan to invade the Soviet Union, Ellison published "Richard Wright and Recent Negro Fiction" in *Direction*, a prestigious journal edited by Kenneth Burke. Although he was growing distant from Wright and from communism, Ellison praised Wright's artistic, intellectual, and emotional power, most evident in his protest novel, *Native Son*. Ellison's 5,000-word essay contrasted Wright's realism to 1920s fiction by other black writers, who had ignored folklore and symbols and the reality of racial discrimination in America. He urged black writers to stop imitating white writers. He called for them to overcome discrimination with an intellectual revolution.

When Hitler broke the terms of his pact with Stalin and invaded the Soviet Union in the summer of 1941, American Communists began to call for the United States to enter World War II. Then, on the morning of December 7, 1941, as German troops were being fought to a standstill a few miles outside of Moscow, Japanese planes launched a surprise bombing attack on the U.S. naval base at Pearl Harbor, Hawaii. The United States was now fighting as an ally of Britain, France, and the Soviet Union.

To mobilize an army, the government began drafting able-bodied men. Ellison did not want to serve in the

A group of Tuskegee Airmen confer over plans during drills at the Tuskegee Army Airfield in Alabama. (Library of Congress)

"Jim Crow" army. To avoid the draft, he tried to claim a medical disability, but the draft board classified him as 1-A, meaning he would be inducted into the army if and when his number was drawn.

To comply with segregation laws, and to avoid antagonizing powerful Southern congressmen, most African Americans in the armed forces were assigned menial jobs as cooks and drivers, instead of duties requiring intellectual or technical skills. The exception was the segregated 66th Air Force Flying School at Tuskegee Institute, which trained black airmen. At first, the airmen were assigned noncombat duty. Later, squadrons participated in raids over Italy and Germany. In spite of their outstanding record during the war, aggressive opposition to integration of the United States Armed Forces continued until 1948, when President Truman finally issued an executive order to end segregation in the military.

Ellison decided to enlist in the merchant marine if he got a draft notice. It was the only branch of service not segregated. Black crewmen could serve in all capacities, even as officers. Even so, his dream of peaceful integration aboard a ship later proved false.

In 1942, as he awaited his draft notice, Ellison was named managing editor of the *Negro Quarterly*, a new journal that published analyses of literature, book reviews, political commentaries, and current events. The *Negro Quarterly* was funded by the Harlem branch of the New York Public Library, the state historical society, the Communist Party, an interracial club, writers' groups, theater groups, and the NAACP.

In addition to writing book reviews and essays, Ellison handled subscriptions, edited submissions, and solicited books to review from publishers. The influence of the Communist Party was still pervasive. Angelo Herndon, a party member, was chief editor and fund-raiser. Ellison had begun to deeply dislike the Communist party line, but their publications provided a market for his work and paid him a salary.

The New York City media had focused on homicides and gang violence committed by blacks, but it did not mention what Ellison considered to be the fundamental causes of crime: squalid living conditions and poverty.

In an essay, "Let Us Consider the Harlem Crime Wave," he described how Harlem residents, with no money to pay utility bills, silently defied white authorities by short-circuiting electric meters in order to have lights, radios, and phonographs. They felt no guilt over using electricity illegally. After all, city workers did not collect their garbage or police their neighborhoods. Later, Ellison used the idea of short-circuiting electricity in his novel *Invisible Man*. The narrator illuminates his underground cavern with stolen electricity that makes his environment visible while he contemplates his future.

In another editorial, "The Way It Is," Ellison interviewed Mrs. Jackson, a Harlem resident. She told how job discrimination had handicapped members of her family. Then she complained about Harlem's high prices for basic necessities, the evictions when the unemployed could not pay rent, the uncollected trash on the sidewalk, crime, police brutality, rampant tuberculosis and venereal disease, and homeless, mentally ill people wandering the streets. In conclusion, Ellison called for price stabilization, rent controls, and greater relief payments to indigent residents.

In an effort to improve the quality of writing submitted to the *Negro Quarterly*, Ellison wrote lengthy critiques of submissions, even if he did not accept them for publication. He recognized wide diversity within the African-American community, related to class, economic status, education, and background. He told prospective writers they should "evaluate [their] experiences from the 'inside,' rather than accept 'outside' analyses." He urged writers not to assume that readers were well-informed about black history or authentic African-American culture. Writers should avoid stereotyping black characters and include more symbols and images of the folklore of African Americans. He liked to publish stories in which optimism triumphed over tragedy. He also preferred that they use colloquial English rather than formal English.

After the *Negro Quarterly* was incorporated into the Negro Publication Society of America, Ellison solicited the work of famous writers, regardless of their ethnicity. Many of the articles had been too radical for the mainstream press. Ellison felt communication between blacks and whites should remain open because black culture was an essential part of American life. As editor, he promoted the idea of "intellectual democracy." Unfortunately, the *Negro Quarterly* went bankrupt, and Ellison had to return to freelancing.

In 1943, when his draft number finally came up, Ellison joined the merchant marine. During the war, he served on freighters carrying ammunition and supplies to troops in Europe. U.S. naval warships accompanied convoys of as many as fifty freighters to protect them from German submarines in the Atlantic Ocean.

Ellison's duties as a cook allowed him time to read and write. He experienced more racism in the merchant marines than he expected, but there was a great deal of freedom from American-style racism in European ports.

This World War II-era recruiting poster for the American Merchant Marine touts the variety of skills and training provided by such service. (Library of Congress)

Unfortunately, drinking water from rusted reserve tanks on the ship caused a recurring kidney infection.

Back in the United States, Ellison usually extended his shore leave as long as he could before the draft board inducted him into the army or sent him to prison. He spent most of his leave at the Vermont home of Stanley Hyman and his wife, Shirley Jackson, author of the famous short story "The Lottery" and the novel *The Haunting of Hill House*. Ellison set up his typewriter in an office in their barn and churned out book reviews and numerous short stories.

"In a Strange County" describes the experience of a black sailor on leave in Wales. While sightseeing, he is harassed and beaten by a group of white American soldiers. Welsh villagers befriend the "Black Yank" and doctor his injuries. Then they play "The Star-Spangled Banner" to show their appreciation for his military service.

This story was published in *Tomorrow* and in *Negro Digest*. Its irony illustrates the bigotry and hatred white American soldiers displayed toward their black comrades. Their behavior contrasts with the stated purpose for the war. They were supposedly fighting a war to free Europeans and restore world peace, even while they were at war with their own countrymen.

The short story "King of the Bingo Game," published in *Tomorrow*, parallels the isolation and helplessness that thousands of unskilled black workers experienced when they moved to northern cities from rural America. In slums and ghettos, they lost contact with their familiar, supportive culture back home. The tragicomic story concerns a friendless and impoverished migrant from the South who desperately needs money for his wife's medical expenses. The man becomes obsessed with playing bingo in hopes that the glitzy wheel, flashing lights, and brash announcer will bring him good fortune. When it doesn't, he becomes hysterical, and policemen raid the hall and beat him senseless.

"Flying Home," another wartime story, was inspired by Ellison's interest in the Tuskegee Airmen. The title is one of Ellison's favorite dance tunes, made famous by his boyhood friend, Charlie Christian, a featured guitarist with Benny Goodman's orchestra. The story illustrates the wide diversity between urban and rural blacks and how they handle a confrontation with a bigoted white man. Todd, a pilot from Tuskegee, flies into a buzzard and crash-lands his airplane on a white man's plantation. Until help arrives, Jefferson, an elderly southern sharecropper, comforts the badly injured pilot by telling him folktales about angels flying free in heaven. Todd thinks the old man is a fool.

When the white plantation owner arrives, he refuses to believe a black man would have the authority to fly a military plane. He threatens to have Todd carted off to a nearby mental hospital in a straight jacket instead of returning him to the Tuskegee air base. Only through Jefferson's clever intervention is the pilot rescued from this racially hostile situation. The white plantation owner remains ignorant of world events that have eroded racial barriers in the South.

The story was published in *Cross Section*, an influential anthology. Ellison was beginning to be better known. Henry Volkening became Ellison's literary agent and was able to secure him a $1,500 advance from the publishers Reynal & Hitchcock for a novel about Todd, the pilot.

While he was home on leave, Ellison enjoyed attending shows at the Apollo and Savoy Theaters, where black singers, dancers, and comedians performed. He went dancing at interracial clubs like the Rhythm Club and Clark Monroe's Uptown House, where the big band sounds of Duke Ellington, Count Basie, and Benny Goodman were at their peak of popularity.

But the Harlem that Ellison had first embraced in

Two African-American marines walk down a busy Harlem street in 1943. (Library of Congress)

1936 was different now. Young migrants from the South had abandoned their rural backgrounds and values. They had come to Harlem in hopes of finding greater freedom and better jobs in defense industries. Instead, they found unemployment, segregation, poverty, gang wars, muggings, murders, and drug deals.

The new social reality created new behaviors and social mores. The new generation was more defiant and less accommodating to racial injustices. These black youth were soon dubbed "hipsters" and actively defied what they considered to be white middle-class values. They wore sunglasses and wide-brimmed hats, and their colorful zoot suits sported exaggerated shoulder pads, wide lapels, knee-length coats, jangling watch chains, and baggy pants snug at the ankle. By exhibiting eccentric behavior and talking jive, many avoided the military draft and were classified 4-F. They felt no obligation to fight for white Europeans' freedom when they had no civil rights in the United States. Newspapers blamed them for the "Negro Crime Wave," but Ellison felt the zoot suit signified another truth. These defiant black youths were weary of being ignored.

After a black soldier was killed by a white policeman, a riot broke out in Harlem. Ellison covered the story for the *New York Post*. His lead was: "When I came out, there was the sound of gunfire and the shouting as of a great celebration." People were venting their rage and frustration over high food prices in their segregated neighborhoods, police brutality, inadequate housing, joblessness, and poverty. It was chaotic. Ellison understood the frustration that led to the riot, but was convinced that the destruction would not bring reform.

In "Richard Wright's Blues," published in *Antioch Review*, Ellison said that *Black Boy*, Wright's fictionalized autobiography, like blues lyrics, gives voice to the suffering within the African-American experience. Wright's genius was his skilled compression of tragedy and optimism, not a psychological examination of his life. Ellison, however, did not agree that life in black communities was culturally barren. African-American culture was a rich part of American culture.

Publication of this essay established Ellison as an

authority on the literature of African-Americans. His reputation as a critic gave him a literary presence independent of Richard Wright's reputation. When critics tried to place them in the same category, Ellison would say, "Wright is by himself. I am by myself. We are individuals."

As World War II drew to a close and the brutality of the Communist dictatorship in the Soviet Union became more evident, Communists in the United States began to leave the party. Members were increasingly viewed as agents of a foreign power. Since Ellison was never an official member, no one noticed his departure.

Richard Wright resigned because the CPUSA had not supported A. Philip Randolph's demand for equal opportunity in wartime industries. Also, he had become interested the Pan-African movement, which upheld the "uniqueness and spiritual unity of black people . . . in all parts of the world." The Communist Party frowned on these cultural and racially based movements. According to the Communists, the only societal role that mattered was if one was a worker. The only identity that an individual should be concerned about, and use to determine his political ideas, was his role in the economy. Wright made his break public in a typically controversial manner by publishing an essay, "I Tried to Be a Communist," in the *Atlantic Monthly*. The essay angered former colleagues at the CPUSA, but it did not stop investigations by the FBI into his political activities. Even such a public rejection did not convince them he was no longer a Communist. Wright moved his family to Paris in 1946. Thereafter, he was no longer considered a popular spokesman for black Americans, although he continued to write a steady stream of criticism about racism in the United States for European newspapers and journals.

In contrast, Ellison's reputation continued to grow. Editors at the *New Republic* asked him to write a commentary on Bucklin Moon's *A Primer for White Folks*, an anthology of essays. Ellison chose the title "Beating That Boy" to signify that he was an African-American insider. During slavery, masters had disciplined workers by beating them. Modern blacks used the phrase when they heard white people stereotyping them and blaming them for racial problems. Before writing the article, Ellison researched negative characterizations of blacks in books and films. He contrasted the American pioneer spirit of freedom and independence with racial segregation and Jim Crow laws.

He had twelve months to finish his novel about Todd from the story "Flying Home." In addition to the advance he got from the publisher, he applied for a Julius Rosenwald Fellowship and received an $1,800 grant. His plan was to have Todd's plane and crew shot down in Germany. In the prison camp, Todd would be the ranking American officer. Nazis would take advantage of the racial antagonism between the white prisoners and their black leader.

But as he struggled to overcome writer's block and get started on the novel, his attention drifted from his planned work to thoughts about the fables of African

Americans, myths about death and rebirth, world history, current events, chaotic life in Harlem, and the South. Little of what Ellison had written so far reflected his own experiences in Oklahoma, Tuskegee, or New York City. He thought it ironic that the high visibility of African Americans actually made black individuals seem invisible to others. Racial stereotyping caused their individuality and diversity to vanish.

He impulsively wrote the words "I am an invisible man." He decided to abandon the novel about Todd, the pilot, and began a new work about a youth "with an infinite capacity for making mistakes."

Seven

THE INVISIBLE
BECOMES VISIBLE

Langston Hughes had introduced Ralph Ellison to Fanny McConnell Buford in 1944. On their first date, Ellison invited her to his apartment to see his library of books and records. He was delighted that she shared his interests in literature, music, politics, and writing. Poised and intelligent, she had a degree in speech and drama from the University of Iowa.

Ellison and Fanny were married in 1946. Langston Hughes served as best man. After their wedding Fanny worked as a secretary while Ellison wrote his book. Each evening, she transcribed and typed his handwritten manuscripts, written on yellow legal pads and sometimes on paper napkins or used envelopes. Never jealous or competitive, she loved him and nurtured his need for isolation when he was working. She was his intellectual equal, the perfect sounding board for his ideas.

To help out with their expenses, Ralph built and installed high-fidelity sound systems for churches and worked as a freelance photographer. When he needed a break from writing, he took his two Scottish terriers for a walk through the noisy, cluttered streets of Harlem.

Writing in their apartment wasn't easy. On one side was a cafe with a loud jukebox, and on the other a tenant who worked nights and played jazz records during the day. Across the courtyard he could hear someone making political speeches and a drunk yelling, "Shut up! Shut up!" Upstairs, a soprano's voice "bounced, ricocheted, whistled, buzzed, wheezed, and trumpeted" through the ceiling.

To counteract her off-key vocalizing, Ellison bought records of Duke Ellington's "Flaming Sword" and Louis Armstrong's "I'll Be Glad When You're Dead, You Rascal, You." When the soprano attempted an aria, he drowned her out with the sound system he had constructed. Her good-natured reaction made him feel guilty. He remembered his own musical beginnings in Oklahoma City and Tuskegee and tried to be more tolerant.

Harlem's alleys were full of drunks, drug addicts, homeless people, and the mentally ill. Ellison wrote an essay called "Harlem Is Nowhere" to publicize the situation and help raise funds for the La Fargue Mental Hygiene Clinic. His friend, psychiatrist Frederic Wertham, operated the clinic in an abandoned church basement. Patients suffering from psychoses and depression paid the clinic twenty-five cents for a consultation.

Wertham theorized that the mental and emotional problems suffered by African Americans were more acute in the North than in the South because southern blacks had developed survival techniques to overcome exploitation and segregation. Their stable religious communities, family institutions, and folk customs—expressed in music, dance, speech, stories, and ethnic foods—sustained them. But when the migrants arrived in northern industrial cities, they found themselves faced with joblessness and poverty without the religious and family ties and social rituals that had sustained them in the South. Some turned to weird religions or alcohol and drugs, or became psychotic.

Ellison collaborated with photographer Gordon Parks on a photo essay about the clinic for *Life* magazine. Parks was a fashion photographer for *Glamour* and *Vogue*, yet his photographs illustrating Ellison's text, showing garbage-strewn alleys and blurred, discouraged faces, were intense and heartrending in their stark, unglamorous realism. Parks was a self-reliant youth from Kansas who had stubbornly refused to submit to Jim Crow restrictions. Before he became a famous photographer, Parks had worked as a musician, waiter, and handyman at an art gallery. Ellison learned about cameras, photography, and film development from Parks.

Ellison took a photograph of Francis Steegmuller, a biographer and translator. When his publisher used the

Gordon Parks is well-known for his fashion, documentary, and civil rights photography shot throughout the twentieth century. This image, taken in Harlem in 1943, is a good example of how his work captures both personality and atmosphere. (Library of Congress)

photograph on a jacket cover for one of his books, Steegmuller offered Ellison use of a quiet office in a wholesale jeweler's suite on he owned Fifth Avenue.

Ellison thought it was ironic that white people on Fifth Avenue and in the elevator of the office building were courteous and never questioned his presence in the upscale neighborhood. In contrast, black people in his St. Nicholas neighborhood in Harlem suspected that he engaged in illegal activities and allowed Fanny to support him. A wino on the corner accused him of being "some kinda sweetback, 'cause...all I ever see [you] do is walk them damn dogs and shoot some damn pictures!"

The Steegmullers also allowed Ellison to use their vacation cabin in Vermont to work on the first chapter of his novel. As he wrote, Ellison found himself returning again and again to his experiences in Deep Deuce and Tuskegee. He had earlier decided the main character would be a naïve but intelligent black youth. He wanted his novel to have a tragicomic tone, metaphors, satire, and ambiguities. Ellison could not restrain his "blues-toned laughter" as he wrote.

In 1947, "Battle Royal," the first chapter from the new novel *Invisible Man,* was published in three different journals. The main character is a naïve teenage African American who is blindfolded during a free-for-all boxing match to entertain a group of white civic leaders. After the match, the bruised and battered boys scramble for fake coins tossed on an electrified rug. The protagonist then delivers a speech about democracy to his insensitive, drunken audience. They award him a college scholarship, which he believes will unlock the door to freedom and success—the first of his many misconceptions.

This excerpt impressed the literary world. Critics thought Ellison had captured the dilemma of black life in America. British readers thought the struggles of the main character revealed the hypocrisy of America's democratic values. Others appreciated Ellison's skillful interior characterization of the black youth. Readers and critics were eager to read the rest of the book.

The success of the excerpt earned the Ellisons some money. They rented a beach house on Long Island. There, with Fanny at his side, Ralph began associating with white artists and intellectuals. At parties, he observed the relative ease with which recent European Jewish immigrants had entered American society. Their friendships were based on mutual interests, not race or gender. Ellison dressed conservatively and used good manners and formal speech. Some new acquaintances assumed the Ellisons were Spanish, a mark of how much Ellison had distanced himself from African-American stereotypes.

Ellison's manuscript was overdue at his publisher because he was a perfectionist. Using his friend Kenneth Burke's theory of "purpose, passion, and perception," he outlined each chapter, trying out different situations before settling on one. He then wrote a draft in longhand and revised it over and over. He hoped to have the "Trueblood" and "Golden Day" episodes published in magazines. He needed money, and he thought publicity would build anticipation for the full novel, but Henry Volkening, his agent, advised against it. He urged Ellison to keep working and to finish the novel.

Ellison struggled with the episodes that dealt with Communist leaders and black nationalists. He wanted to show how political leaders, both black and white, used civil rights issues to gain power while ignoring the real concerns of African Americans.

Ellison opposed the ideology of black nationalism, which held that African Americans would never be truly free until they had a separate black nation of their own. In the novel, he presented Ras the Exhorter as a heroic black nationalist leading his "warriors" with antiquated weapons. He saw black nationalism as being futile and unrealistically romantic.

Ellison was an authority on race riots in the United States. He had researched the topic extensively, beginning with the riot in Tulsa. He wanted the novel to show that rioting brings chaos to a community by destroying lives and property without leading to reform.

While struggling with the final episode, when the youth goes "underground," he began revision on earlier episodes of *Invisible Man*, which was now over 886 manuscript pages long. During the revision, Stanley Hyman and Shirley Jackson helped him reduce it to 612 pages. Jackson was especially good at suggesting transitions from one scene to another.

Langston Hughes teased Ellison about the length of his novel-in-progress. Ellison described it as a blues tale with tragic elements but said that it had an optimistic conclusion that left the main character with infinite possibilities. He explained its theme as a black man's search for identity in a hostile, indifferent world.

Ellison worried how some contemporary African-American critics, such as the young and sharp-tongued James Baldwin, would react to *Invisible Man*. He knew

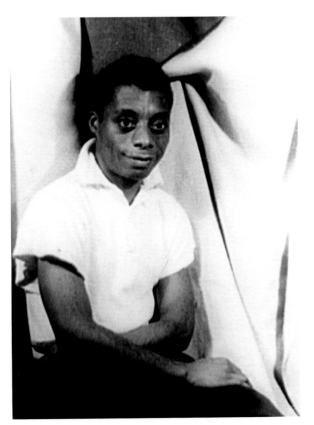

Writer, critic, and civil rights activist James Baldwin. (Library of Congress)

that although Richard Wright had helped Baldwin get a Rosenwald Fellowship, Baldwin had written derisive essays about *Native Son*. Baldwin disliked Wright's presentation of African Americans as victims, unable to escape their dilemma.

Ellison admitted *Invisible Man* "did protest the agony of growing up in a complex society. It did protest clichés about African-Americans in traditional literature. It did protest human vulnerability when confronted by physical, intellectual, military, or legal antagonists." However, he intended the novel to go beyond mere protest. He wanted his book to have universal appeal.

Invisible Man showed how the denial of a person's individuality was the most oppressive and damaging aspect of racial intolerance and segregation. However, instead of publishing another protest novel about how racism destroyed the individual, Ellison wanted his hero to escape destructive societal pressures. He thought his own experience showed that introspection and self-analysis could allow individuals to correct their errors in judgment, and make a fresh start. Wise choices and personal goals could transcend social barriers.

This emphasis on the individual creating his or her own reality separate from socially assigned roles was part of the postwar interest in the philosophy called existentialism, which had been popularized primarily by the French writers Albert Camus and Jean-Paul Sartre. In addition to this existential theme, the novel could be interpreted on other levels. After its publication, Ellison said *Invisible Man* was about "innocence, human error, a struggle through illusion to reality." He said it had many layers of interest: psychological, literary, ritualistic, mythological, and historical. He pointed out his use of "naturalism, expressionism, and surrealism to express the [main character's] state of consciousness and the state of society." He also told reporters the book was about the failure of leadership, a theme many reviewers overlooked. When they asked him if the novel was autobiographical, he replied, "Well, let's put it this way, [it] all happened to me—in my head, [in my] imagination."

Ellison corresponded regularly with Albert Murray, a professor at Tuskegee and an officer in the Air Force Reserves. They had been casual acquaintances at Tuskegee but became close friends in 1950 while Murray was in graduate school at New York University. Ellison confided to Murray that the novel could be interpreted as "a big fat ole Negro lie, meant to be told during cotton picking time over a water bucket full of corn, with a dipper passing back and forth at a good fast clip so that no one, not even the narrator himself, will realize how utterly preposterous the lie actually is." Still, Ellison insisted there was a truth about life embedded in the heart of his story. He described his writing style as that of a jazz musician improvising on the novel's basic existential theme with a "wild star-burst of metamorphosis."

As the novel slowly neared completion, his editor, Albert Erskine, began to help with revision. Meeting at Erskine's home, they cut many scenes and eliminated some of the more obscure symbols. Ellison worked on dialogue to make it sound like authentic speech. He read his words into a tape recorder and played it back to listen for rhythm and sound.

On February 4, 1952, seven years after Ellison had first written the lines, "I am an invisible man. . . . I am invisible because people refuse to see me," advance copies of *Invisible Man* were sent to critics. The jacket cover showed the mask of a human face, designed by the expressionist artist E. McKnight Kauffer. On the

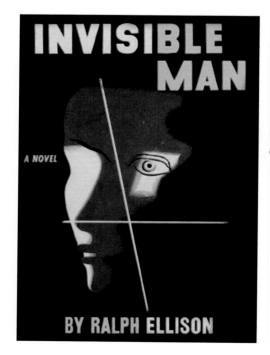

The original 1952 jacket cover of Invisible Man.

back was a photograph of Ellison by Gordon Parks. Ralph dedicated the novel to Ida, his mother.

Most critics gave the novel excellent reviews. One compared Ellison to the classic poet Homer, who defined the ancient Greek cultural identity in the *Iliad* and the *Odyssey*. Ellison identified the strengths and weaknesses of African-American culture from an inside point of view, which made *Invisible Man* unique in American fiction. Former teachers and contemporary writers sent congratulatory letters. Bookstores sold every copy and ordered more. *Invisible Man* made the *New York Times* best-seller list for sixteen weeks. The publisher had it translated into several languages. Ellison became famous in literary circles and received invitations to lecture at universities and write essays on race relations.

But not everyone appreciated the novel. LeRoi Jones, who would later change his name to Amiri Baraka, was then a young political activist and writer. Jones said Ellison had betrayed the African-American community because his hero avoids conflicts. John Killens, founder of the Harlem Writers Guild and a labor activist, called *Invisible Man* a "vicious distortion of Negro life."

These critics demanded solidarity and conformity among African Americans in the battle for civil rights, and Ellison had not adhered to their point of view. Although he was certain about his aesthetic vision, the criticisms stung. He explained repeatedly that he never intended *Invisible Man* to be a protest novel. He wanted it to have a universal message, to show how individuals can find identity and purpose within a hostile environment. He tried to show the values and ethics people must develop when faced with marvelous and terrible obstacles. "Marvelous refers to the triumph of the human spirit over chaos, and terrible refers to all that hinders or oppresses human aspirations." Ellison believed in the power of individuals to resolve conflicts. This was contrary to his critics' more militant ideology, which demanded a single black voice. Ellison had found a way to let his individual voice as a writer find expression, and that was considered politically suspect by many activists.

Eight

APPLAUSE AND NOSTALGIA

Ellison received the National Book Award's gold medal for fiction on January 27, 1953, at a ceremony held at the Commodore Hotel in New York City. The only criterion for the honor was that the work of literature had to reflect the state of American art and writing. He was the first African American to win this prestigious award. The runner-up was *The Old Man and the Sea*, by Ernest Hemingway, an author whose work Ellison admired.

To promote *Invisible Man*, Ellison's acceptance speech was broadcast on radio prior to the ceremony, and he was interviewed on the *Today* television show. Interviewers asked him why the main character declared he was invisible when his skin color made him highly visible. Ellison explained that segregation denied vis-

Frederick Lewis Allen (second from left), *editor of* Harper's Magazine, *presents the 1953 National Book Awards in New York City. Ellison stands at the far left. Fellow award-winners Benard De Voto and Archibald MacLeish stand to the right.* (AP Photo/John Rooney)

ibility to individual blacks. Many white people lumped African Americans culturally, physically, and psychologically into one group and refused to see them as separate individuals with diverse qualities and talents. Ironically, many of his black critics also attacked his emphasis on individual, instead of group, identity.

At the awards ceremony, Ellison looked slender and athletic in a white dress shirt, dark tie, and conservative blue suit. Fanny noted how her husband carefully combed his hair to cover his bald spot, a reminder that he was now thirty-nine.

He began his speech by telling the audience that his parents had named him Ralph Waldo Ellison because they hoped he would become an author like his namesake. Then he described his journey from being a musician to becoming a writer. He talked about how fiction should reveal the truth of the human condition, just as children's fairy tales reveal a kernel of truth about human behavior. He admitted that his novel was experimental, that with its moral themes it was more like nineteenth-century fiction than twentieth-century fiction, which, he said, seldom portrays the full complexity of American life. He explained that he had used a blend of "folk, Biblical, scientific, and political language" to express the sound of his characters' diverse speech patterns. Then he gave credit to the other writers who had influenced him.

Also receiving recognition that night was Bernard De Voto, the nonfiction award winner, and Archibald MacLeish for poetry. Supreme Court Justice William O. Douglas was in the audience, and Ellison was amused when Douglas asked him if he had graduated from the University of Oklahoma. Until 1948, when law student Ada Lois Sipuel dared cross the color line to enroll, the university had been an all-white institution.

A cash prize of $1,000 allowed Ralph and Fanny to lease an apartment on Riverside Drive overlooking the

Hudson River. Through his binoculars, Ellison could watch children playing basketball in the park, and on the hi-fi equipment he had constructed he could listen to his collection of blues and jazz records.

Royalties from book sales gave him a steady income for the first time in his life. No longer pressed for money, Ellison spent his leisure time enjoying several hobbies. He collected books, took and developed photographs, and collected Kachina dolls (made of cottonwood by the Hopi and Zuni tribes), African carvings, sculpture, and paintings. He grew African violets and designed furniture. He had a talking parakeet and a Labrador named Tuckatarby that he took for daily walks. When visitors came, Ellison would light a cigar and carry on a leisurely conversation.

However, the rest of the world was not so peaceful. America was engaged in a "Cold War" with Russia, and an invisible "Iron Curtain" isolated Soviet dominated Eastern Europe from the West. Anyone in the Soviet Union who opposed the Communist Party's authority was sent to a labor camp or executed. Communist inspired revolutions in China and North Korea had established totalitarian regimes. British and French Empires were crumbling, leaving social chaos and the threat of new wars.

In the United States, black veterans returning from the Korean War felt betrayed by segregation and job discrimination. They began demanding their civil rights. The revolutionary international Pan-African movement called for people of color throughout the world to unite against European colonialism in Africa. Richard Wright and other members of the movement coined the term negritude, to express a sense of black consciousness and black power.

Ellison was still in touch with his old friend Langston Hughes. In 1953, Hughes was called to testify before Senator Joseph McCarthy's Un-American Activities Committee, which was grabbing headlines by accusing prominent writers, film makers, and other intellectuals of being secret Communist agents. McCarthy saw the opportunity presented by fear of Communist expansion

Langston Hughes speaks before the House Un-American Activities Committee in Washington, D.C., on March 26, 1953. Hughes testified before the Senate investigations subcommittee that he had formerly been sympathetic to the Soviet form of government but had never joined the Communist Party. Hughes did not name names. (AP Photo)

to promote his own career. His committee's stated goal was to expose traitors who were distributing Communist propaganda through books, film, and broadcasts. Two of Hughes' books were on the blacklist, which led publishers to reject Hughes's work. These charges stemmed from radical poetry he had written during a tour of the Soviet Union in 1932, twenty years before. The poems had condemned racism and religion in the United States and advocated revolution as a radical solution. Hughes now called himself a "sharecropper poet" because he wrote in a variety of genres to support himself—plays, opera librettos, song lyrics, children's stories, and a newspaper column.

The Ellisons stood by their old friend, offering him moral support and encouragement. Ellison urged Hughes to invigorate his career by writing about his friendships with world-famous writers such as Arthur Koestler, Nicolas Guillen, Federico Garcia Lorca, and Ernest Hemingway. In his easygoing way, Hughes replied, "If I wrote the book you want me to write, people wouldn't buy it, and I would have to take a job."

Hughes owned a three-story boarding house in Harlem. He and Ellison discussed the changes taking place in the area and the way the contemporary jazz scene reflected the changing, chaotic world. Referring to modern bebop jazz, so named for the sounds a saxophone or trumpet can make, Ellison compared life in Harlem to a bebop jam session. He thought bebop was symbolic of a deep alienation within African-American

Despite some progress in racial integration, Oklahoma City's streetcar network and school system were still starkly segregated when Ellison visited in the early 1950s. (Library of Congress)

culture because it was no longer connected to the original identity of blues and jazz that had emerged from places like Deep Deuce.

In 1953, Ellison returned to Oklahoma City to attend a cousin's funeral. While he was there, Jimmy Stewart took him on a tour of the city. Ellison was pleased that housing segregation had eased somewhat and that "Mose [was] living within spitting distance of the capital and the white folks [were] accepting our presence with a certain amount of grace." (When he talked with or wrote to close friends, Ellison always used the word "moses" or "mose" to describe himself and others as "down home folks.")

Ellison visited his father's grave at a beautifully

landscaped cemetery where pioneer families were buried. Thirty-six years before, he remembered the site as "raw, red clay mounds with crude granite stones [surrounded by] wild countryside."

Old friends welcomed him. They flocked around him and called him "Raf." He said they made him feel like a "red-cock crowing on a hill." The familiar setting reminded him of his boyhood, when he was "living in that earlier time, in that old house where my cousin lived when we were young, hearing the old rain in the night, the old thunder, the old lightning, and in the morning the hens sang soft beneath my window." Seeing Deep Deuce again inspired him to write "Deep Second," a rare, sentimental poem about his youth. Later, he wrote to Albert Murray: "I've got one Oklahoma book in me, I do believe."

Although Ellison was gratified that racial segregation in Oklahoma City had declined, he was skeptical and wary that social transitions would be as smooth elsewhere. In 1954, the Supreme Court ruled that segregation in public schools was unconstitutional. This event helped to set off a civil rights movement that transformed American society over the next two decades. After the decision, Ellison became more optimistic, but he thought black leaders, such as Roy Wilkins at the NAACP, were naive in assuming new civil rights laws would end segregation and racism. Segregation still permeated American society at its deepest roots. Change would have to come from the heart of millions of individuals, both black and white.

Nine

CHANGE THE JOKE AND SLIP THE YOKE

In 1955, the American Academy of Arts and Letters awarded Ellison the Prix de Rome, which provides a scholarship to study classical literature, lecture, and write in the Italian capital. He and Fanny sailed aboard the USS *Constitution* to spend a year in Italy. They lived in a villa with a vegetable and flower garden. Ellison thought some of his scholarly neighbors were snobbish, but he won bets with them on Sugar Ray Robinson's boxing matches. While he studied and planned his lectures, Fanny saw the sights in Rome. She also worked part time for a Catholic relief organization.

They had anticipated a pleasant year, but before it was over they were both ready to "give Rome back to the Etruscans." They disliked the humid climate and pollution on the streets. Fanny suffered an attack of

Ellison at his typewriter during his American Academy of Arts and Letters scholarship in Rome. (AP Photo)

appendicitis, and Ralph came down with pneumonia.

During this time, Albert Murray was stationed with the U.S. Air Force in Casablanca. In letters, Ellison jokingly warned Murray not to wear white or the Arabs would claim him as a brother. Homesick, he asked Murray to send him some new tapes of the Duke Ellington and Count Basie orchestras. He confided that he missed "cornbread, sweet potatoes, black-eyed peas, biscuits, and real greens."

While in Italy, Ellison wrote "Society, Morality, and the Novel," an essay that discussed how novels can lead to social change. Communication between author and reader depends upon shared assumptions about reality, he wrote. Settings should have universal significance. The reader must identify with the main character's experiences, either in real life or in the reader's imagination. Word choices and use of figures of speech, like metaphors or symbols, contribute to a reader's vision of scenes and action.

Ellison's musical background made him conscious of the importance of transitions between scenes and changes of mood, as well as the sound of words in dialogue. He credited James Joyce and T. S. Eliot for showing him how to use a wide range of language. He credited the French novelist Andre Malraux with emphasizing the worth of an individual within a culture or political system, and Fyodor Dostoyevsky with contrasting characters from different levels of society. He had wanted his novel to give insight into the life of an African-American youth as he searched for his identity and emerged from a chaotic situation with a new perspective on his future.

American writers Nathaniel Hawthorne, Herman Melville, Henry James, and Mark Twain had presented psychological insights and moral themes that were influential in the development of the nation. They indicated changes in society, the breakup of traditions, and the effects of new technology. They also revealed the importance of the Declaration of Independence, the Constitution, and the Bill of Rights as rational solutions for chaotic situations.

In contrast, Ellison said many modern novels had no answer for "irrational social change and chaos." A great novel is "a rational art form for dealing with the irrational, and well-written fiction can give insights into social conflicts." He admired the work of his contemporaries Saul Bellow and William Faulkner, both of whom confronted moral issues in their work.

Black artists and intellectuals who characterized African Americans in a negative way particularly annoyed Ellison. He asked, "How did these critics escape their racial heritage?" He accused them of accepting simple formulas to cure racism in America and allowing social scientists to interpret their lives.

One of the intellectuals whose work he opposed was Gunnar Myrdal, a Swedish social scientist and author of *An American Dilemma*. Myrdal theorized that African Americans were predestined to poverty and low social status because of their past history of slavery. Ellison angrily rejected Myrdal's thesis. He believed African Americans should refuse to remain victims of the past. They should take pride in their contributions to American culture and assume responsibility for the future.

In 1958, Ellison published "Change the Joke and Slip the Yoke" in the *Partisan Review*. The title is from an old slave proverb, signifying that a smile and a clever story can hide a slave's deception and win him a degree of freedom from his master. The essay was in rebuttal to Stanley Hyman's "The Promised Land," a discussion of literary archetypes. The two men were friends who enjoyed a good argument.

Their debate centered on the significance of the blackface minstrel show, which was popular in the United States until the 1950s, when it was finally recognized as bigotry, not comedy. Originally, the minstrel show

This 1899 minstrel-show poster depicts the popular yet extremely problematic blackface portrayal of African-American men, over which Ellison and Stanley Hyman debated. (Library of Congress)

was performed by white men in blackface makeup and colorful costumes. They lampooned African Americans with songs, dances, and jokes. Stock characters were Jim Crow, a carefree slave, Mr. Tambo, the tambourine man, and Zip Coon, a freed slave pretending to be a "gentleman." In the 1920s, black actors began playing the parts using Negro dialect. The ensemble sang and played banjos, fiddles, tambourines, and bone castanets.

Hyman claimed the blackface minstrel was based on an African archetype, the trickster—a playful, sometimes dangerous character who questions the norms and rituals of a society. Ellison disagreed. He said minstrels' blackface makeup, red, white, and blue costumes, and their songs, dances, and jokes reflected white Americans' moral, political, and social conflicts toward blacks. Minstrel shows served as "comic catharsis" for whites and a source of humiliation for blacks.

Ellison claimed blacks have always worn masks to try out new possibilities while protecting their real thoughts and feelings. His own grandfather had worn a mask of conformity to protect his family. Louis Armstrong's mask of sweat, spit, and grimaces had allowed him to poke fun at important people, even presidents, without offending them. Armstrong's skill as a musician had won him fame and fortune from white audiences. For that reason, many misguided African Americans maligned him as not being authentically black.

Ellison argued that most people, regardless of race, wear masks to hide their emotions and intentions: "The smart man playing dumb [is] not necessarily a Negro strategy. . . . America is a land of masking jokers." Ellison admitted he had worn a minstrel mask as he wrote *Invisible Man*. His mask was constructed of literary techniques of allegory, symbolism, understatement, allusions, double entendre, satire, and signifying. Wearing the narrator's mask had allowed him a "long, loud rant, howl, and laugh" before he removed it at the end.

In 1958, the Ellisons moved to a large farmhouse in the Catskill Mountains near Bard College, where Ralph had been offered a teaching position. He loved the seclusion of the home he called Larrabee Farm, but suffered from hay fever. During the week, Fanny commuted to New York to work as a fund-raiser for a medical missionary. They shared the house with Saul Bellow,

The pastoral views and peaceful surroundings of the Catskills gave Ellison a much-needed break from city life during his teaching stint at Bard College. (Library of Congress)

author of *The Adventures of Augie March*, a novel that won the National Book Award in 1954. Bellow was also a professor at Bard.

Due to their teaching schedules and need for solitude to write, the two men rarely saw each other, except at breakfast. According to Bellow, Ellison wore a colorful bathrobe and house shoes with turned-up toes and had an annoying habit of massaging his nose and cracking its cartilage while he waited for coffee to brew. During breaks from planning lectures and working on his second novel, Ellison smoked his pipe, did the laundry, prepared meals, changed the oil in his old Chrysler, and took his Labrador for a walk. He also took photographs and watered his African violets. On Wednesday nights, he went to a tavern in town, where he ate supper and danced with students to music from a jukebox. Crowds gathered to see Ellison "dance the chicks bowlegged."

Ellison and Bellow occasionally had cocktails together and shared ideas and read their manuscripts aloud. Ellison confided that his goal had been to write an insider's perspective of African-American culture. Bellow said his goal had been to write an insider's perspective of the Jewish-American community. Although they had not previously discussed writing strategies, some of their short-story characters faced similar problems. Although both had rejected communism as a political ideology, they thought of themselves as leftists because the right side of the political spectrum had not accepted racial equality and equal

Ralph Ellison

Novelist Saul Bellow would go on to win the Nobel Prize in Literature in 1976. (Library of Congress)

economic opportunity as two of its objectives.

Both men were from ethnic minorities. Throughout history, religious and cultural bias against Jews and racial and cultural bias against African Americans were tremendous obstacles. When a critic later described Ellison as "a black Jew," he replied, "All us old-fashioned Negroes are Jews." He meant that African Americans identify with Old Testament stories about Jewish captivity and enslavement and their resiliency during times of persecution.

At Bard, Ellison taught American literature and Russian novels. Remembering how he had not been allowed to debate issues with professors at Tuskegee, he encouraged students to ask questions. Sometimes he read episodes of his novel-in-progress aloud. Students were fascinated by the rhythm and sound of the words.

He was surprised that they knew so little about the real history of blacks in America. He told them how a variety of different tribes and cultures had been brought from Africa to America as slaves after 1620. Many intermarried with European immigrants and Native Americans. After the Civil War, they had adopted values that the U.S. Constitution promised to all its citizens. However, customs and laws in many states refused to give black Americans their civil rights. As a result, they endured discrimination and economic turmoil. To avoid suffering and tragedy when racial confrontations became violent, they often reverted to passive roles.

Ellison emphasized that in spite of political and social handicaps, African Americans had contributed greatly to speech, food, clothing, dance, art, sports, literature, religion, and music that "makes life swing." He believed the American cultural "melting pot" made segregation impossible to maintain, not only for white segregationists but also for black nationalists.

In 1955, African Americans began to engage in a series of nonviolent demonstrations to claim their civil rights, beginning with the bus boycotts in Montgomery, Alabama, led by a young preacher named Martin Luther King Jr. Over the next decade, the movement began to win converts and to force the issue of racial injustice onto American television screens and into newspapers. King emerged as the leader of this nonviolent movement. In 1963, he inspired millions with his "I Have a Dream" speech, delivered during the massive March on

Washington. In retaliation, white segregationists initiated legal challenges that soon escalated into harassment, vandalism, bombings, and murder.

Ellison attended rallies and contributed money to support sit-ins, but he was reluctant to join any group that expected him to conform without question to its leadership. From childhood, he had avoided direct racial confrontations. Instead, he favored Martin Luther King's technique of nonviolence.

Ellison regarded the Constitution as the "vital covenant by which Americans of diverse backgrounds, religions, races, and interests [are] bound." However, slavery was the "crack in the Liberty Bell . . . a serpentlike malignancy that split America's ideals of equality and freedom into issues of color and race." He especially liked the line in the Pledge of Allegiance: "One nation, indivisible, with liberty and justice for all."

As the civil rights movement progressed into the late 1960s, militant black nationalists threatened violence. Stokely Carmichael and others urged African Americans to reject integration and to form an all-black coalition. They adopted a strategy used during slavery days, which was to shun anyone who went outside the black community and associated with whites. In the militants' eyes Ellison was one of the traitors who refused to conform to the militant idea of how a black intellectual and artist should live and work. For his part, Ellison disapproved of the speaking style of black nationalists such as Malcolm X, one of the leaders of the Nation of

Black nationalist leader Malcolm X at a 1964 press conference, less than a year before he was assassinated. (Library of Congress)

Islam, who "talked a lot but accomplished little." He described Malcolm X's speaking style as "pulpit exhortation, combined with pool hall and barbershop rhetoric." It raised the consciousness of black audiences, but it also raised the consciousness of white racists who burned churches and lynched people.

When militants reviled Ellison for not joining them in marches and demonstrations, he replied that he was a writer, not an activist. Ellison did not support the Black Arts Movement (BAM) or black power nationalism, because he felt these ideologies isolated black artists and intellectuals and kept them from attaining recognition in American music, art, politics, education, sports, and literature.

Critics accused him of being a token representative for African Americans because he served on important national committees with whites. He jokingly offered to put a cardboard cutout in his place, but asked his detractors who would look after their interests if he resigned, or who would even remember that they existed.

Ellison became a target of insults when he spoke on college campuses across the nation. Outwardly, he seemed impassive toward these personal attacks, but his insistence that American black culture had blended into American white culture offended young black nationalists, who viewed black culture as separate from the broader American culture. One young woman said, "That just proves you're an Uncle Tom," meaning he had betrayed those who depended upon his leadership.

President Lyndon B. Johnson signed the Civil Rights Act of 1964, which outlawed legal segregation in public facilities throughout the United States. Johnson asked artists and intellectuals like Ellison to help "dissolve the barriers of hatred and ignorance, which are the source of so much of our [nation's] pain and danger."

Ten

JAZZ

Ralph Ellison never abandoned his love for blues and jazz. It was food for his soul. He kept up with friends from his boyhood, Charlie Christian and Jimmy Rushing, who lived in Harlem, and he knew all of the big-time jazzmen and blues singers. During the decades between 1940 and 1970, the music scene in America changed. Ellison thought it reflected a transformation in American culture. Because many magazine editors considered him an authority on blues and jazz, they often asked him to write about music.

Ellison's training as a musician made him a perceptive critic. He considered jazz a unique American art form, a hybrid made by combining marches, ragtime, blues, classical music, and spirituals. He recognized a jazz performance as a ritual, requiring physical and emotional expression, shown by the way musicians held their instruments, their body language, and their facial expressions. To be good, the music had to communicate a mood to dancers on the floor.

He wrote about Minton's Playhouse. In the 1940s, Minton's had been a shrine for jazz musicians. After the last shows were over in the Harlem theater district, Henry Minton customarily served a huge supper to musicians, singers, dancers, and show business celebrities. He managed the office and served as many performers' booking agent. He loaned money to and fed unemployed musicians, and provided them a place to jam. The house band consisted of trumpeter Dizzy Gillespie, drummer Kenny Clarke, guitarist Charlie Christian, pianist Thelonious Monk, alto saxophonist Charlie Parker, and singer Jimmy Rushing. "It was a place that was jumping with good times," Ellison wrote.

Musicians came from all over the world to sit in with these jazzmen. They sometimes shared their techniques with aspiring novices who had to undergo "apprentice-ships, ordeals, initiation ceremonies, and rebirth [of soul] in order to meet the group's standards." A musician could be challenged and replaced by someone with more soul, or better technique, in the use of a mute, intonations, or pitch.

In "The Golden Age, Time Past" for *Esquire* maga-zine, Ellison refuted the myth that modern jazz musi-cians "found" their art at Minton's Playhouse. This incorrect "history [of modern jazz is] a tall tale told by

From left to right: *jazz pianist Thelonious Monk, trumpeter Howard McGhee, Minton's Playhouse manager Teddy Hill, and trumpeter Roy Eldridge outside Minton's at West 118th Street in New York City.* (AP Photo)

inattentive idealists." Before jazzmen dominated the scene at Minton's, black musicians met in places like Hallie Richardson's shoe-shine parlor in Oklahoma City or similar places in southern or midwestern towns. There, they worked up intricate improvisations in small, private jam sessions. Blues and jazz moved to clubs and dance halls, where people acted out their feelings on the dance floor and "musical instruments were locked in a passionate recitative. The traditional jazz beat and blues mood swept [across America] like a great river from its old, deep bed."

One of Ellison's favorite jazzmen was Louis Armstrong, who understood that "the real secret of the game [was] to make life swing." To communicate with

Jazz trumpeter Louis Armstrong popularized scat singing. (Library of Congress)

an audience during a set, Satchmo, as he was called, might combine snatches of Verdi and Broadway ballads mixed in with jazz standards. In his gravelly voice, he often sang scat (nonsense syllables) to a basic melody. During the bebop era, when the Minton musicians and others created modern jazz, many young jazzmen disliked Armstrong and called him an "Uncle Tom" because he was so popular with white people.

The most famous founders of bebop jazz were Charlie "Bird" Parker on alto saxophone, Dizzy Gillespie on trumpet, and Kenny Clarke on drums. They considered themselves artists, not entertainers. Some "boppers" had formal musical training, and their focus was on experimental interpretation, not tradition. They resented all-white dance bands that performed on the radio and in hotel ballrooms, where black musicians were not allowed, so they often turned their backs on white audiences to show their contempt. They deliberately introduced intricate changes (chord progressions and inversions) so white musicians could not copy their style.

Ellison disliked bebop because it had no danceable rhythm. He described it as "mechanistic, repetitive, nervous, not fully formed . . . secret and taunting . . . flat or shrill. . . . Its rhythms were out of stride and seemingly arbitrary . . . the revolutionary rumpus sounding like a series of flubbed notes." He claimed that bebop had a despairing tone, that it was "fragmented, chaotic, and pretentious" and reflected chaotic life in America caused by social upheavals and wars.

In 1962, Ellison wrote "On Bird, Bird-Watching, and Jazz" for *Saturday Review*. He began by asking a rhetorical question: "What kind of 'bird' was Charlie 'Bird' Parker?" "Bird" was famous for his fast, complex improvisations. Birdland, the famous jazz club, was decorated with birdcages and named for him. Oddly, most jazzmen were called "cats," not "birds." Ellison compared Bird to a mockingbird that mimics other birdcalls and warbles a wide range of notes, phrases, and repetitions.

Parker's wild, self-destructive escapades under the influence of alcohol and drugs made him all the more attractive to his imitators and those who looked up to him. Long after his death in 1955, fans scrawled "Bird

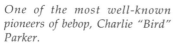

One of the most well-known pioneers of bebop, Charlie "Bird" Parker.

Lives!" on buildings, freight trains, and underpasses. Bebop jazz inspired writers like Jack Kerouac, Allen Ginsberg, and others of the so-called "Beat Generation," who tried to write poetry and prose with erratic rhythms that mimicked the new jazz.

After attending the Newport Jazz Festival, Ellison wrote Albert Murray, "The cats have gotten lost, man," signifying the quality of jazz had declined. To Ellison, hard bop, disconnected from dancing and vocalizing, lacked "soul." It had become "the frantic shriek of a lost, big-citified people whose home [was] nowhere."

In a 1964 *New York Review*, Ellison wrote that *Blues People*, a book by Amiri Baraka, was so negative and militant that it "gave even the blues the blues." Baraka claimed that blacks had played the "blues" since slavery and that this genre expressed their continued repression in America.

To Ellison, Baraka's claim that black culture had been

repressed for one hundred years was wrong. Blues, jazz, and gospel music, and the artists who created it, were such an integral part of twentieth-century American culture that "styles of dancing, speaking, dressing, sports [were all] jazz-shaped."

Intellectuals tried to place Ellison, Richard Wright, and other black writers in a genre of literature called the Blues School. Ellison refused the association. "There is no Blues School," he declared. However, he did not deny the relationship between the blues and his work. He defined blues as the "impulse to keep painful details and episodes of a brutal experience alive in one's aching consciousness, to finger its jagged grain, and to transcend it, not by the consolation of philosophy, but by squeezing from it a near tragic, near comic lyricism. As a form, the blues is an autobiographical chronicle of personal catastrophe expressed lyrically."

Ellison admired Duke Ellington's elegant style and how he had incorporated the blues rhythms into his suave and sophisticated music. He had once dreamed of composing danceable blues and jazz music for a tuxedo-clad orchestra. He was upset when the Pulitzer Prize committee denied Ellington an award for his composition "Black and Tan Fantasy," with its dark, emotional themes overlaid with lighthearted dance rhythms. Ellison thought "Fantasy" blended the best of African-American blues with snatches of classical concertos. He thought Ellington was America's greatest composer and appreciated how he had learned to wear an "enigmatic, smiling mask" as he watched hundreds of white high school and college youth dance to his music. His popularity and grace mocked the legitimacy of segregation.

Ellison's essays and stories about music have an authoritative, insider's tone. They reveal a personality entirely different from the critic who would sometimes harshly review books and articles. While he was working on a project, he listened to a large collection of records on the sound system he had built himself. Sometimes he played his trumpet when he suffered from writer's block, as music continued to be his creative muse.

Eleven

JUNETEENTH

I n 1964, Ellison spoke to an audience at the Library of Congress. His address was entitled "Hidden Name and Complex Fate." He told how his father had believed in the power of a name, a custom many black parents followed by naming their children after famous people. He admitted that he had once detested his name but felt obligated to live up to it. With a smile, he said that even though his namesake had been dead since 1882, he occasionally received mail addressed to Mr. Ralph Waldo Emerson.

Names, he said, are symbolic of family values and traditions, yet they may also hide the identity of the real person. For example, a black American spy during the Revolutionary War took the name James Armistead Lafayette to honor the French general. Some slaves accepted their owner's name, like Ellison's grandfather Alfred Ellison or Jefferson Davis (J. D.) Randolph. After emancipation, others rejected these slave names and adopted new ones.

Ellison said names connect us to the world around us. To explain, he used the analogy of the Tar Baby and Bre'r Rabbit, a folktale. The world, like the Tar Baby, is unresponsive to an individual's struggle to find freedom. We, like Bre'r Rabbit, accept the world's opinion of who we are and get stuck.

To break free from the world's opinion of what a black man should be, Ellison credited his lifelong reading habit, the rich language and folktales he heard in Oklahoma City, excellent teachers of literature, classical and jazz musicians, movies, sports, foods, dancing, and acquaintances with people of different ethnic backgrounds. Becoming a writer had been a slow process of self-discovery.

In 1964, Random House published *Shadow and Act*, a collection of essays written over the previous twenty-two years. The essays contain autobiographical facts. "Shadow" in the title refers to Ellison's past experiences, which foreshadowed his "act" as a writer. The essays can be grouped into three of his areas of expertise: literature and folklore, jazz and blues, and African-American culture. Most had been published previously in magazines.

Ellison's long essay, "The World and the Jug," is written in two sections. The first is in reaction to white critic Irving Howe's 1963 essay "Black Boys and Native

Ralph Ellison is photographed here at the Random House offices in February of 1964. (AP Photo)

Sons." The second part is Ellison's reply to what Howe had written to rebut the first part of the essay. He combined them in the final published version.

Ellison was particularly offended by Howe's tone of superiority toward those writers he alluded to as "black boys," namely James Baldwin and himself. Howe, an admirer of Richard Wright's protest novel *Native Son*, claimed black writers had a duty to protest the pain and suffering they endured because of racism. Otherwise, they would not represent their experiences truthfully. He accused Ellison and Baldwin of betraying Wright, the man who had influenced their early careers, by not protesting racial injustice more vigorously.

Ellison had always acknowledged Wright's role in helping him become a writer. However, he did reject Wright's characterization of Bigger Thomas, the uneducated, inarticulate protagonist of *Native Son*, as a representative black man. He believed that novels should "celebrate human life . . . preserve as they destroy, and affirm as they reject." His own goal in *Invisible Man* had been to give readers insight into the mind of a youth struggling to find his identity in a hostile world, not to protest the past.

He explained his essay's title, "The World and the Jug," by saying that he wanted freedom in the world, not confinement in "an opaque steel jug with the Negroes inside waiting for some black messiah to come along and blow the cork."

Ellison claimed that each black writer projects a unique point of view. He used his favorite words—complexity and diversity—to describe black people's experiences in America. The idea that all African Americans are basically the same denies their individuality. What they do have in common is their cultural heritage, their history of slavery, emancipation, betrayal during

Reconstruction, segregation, and the influence of European immigrants. Out of this heritage, individuals can discover unique possibilities.

He noted those black intellectuals and artists who gain recognition develop self-control and know how to turn aside racial slurs. They deal with harsh realities of life with courage and are willing to create art out of their personal, often painful, experiences. They refuse to be victims. Their merit rests on their artistic skills and accomplishments. He named Leontyne Price (the opera singer), Duke Ellington, Louis Armstrong, and Richard Wright as examples of artists who had developed insights and strategies to overcome obstacles and to attain a rich life.

In part two of the essay, Ellison used his own life to illustrate how he had escaped the "opaque jug." In his youth, he knew he could do nothing to change Jim Crow restrictions, so he developed other interests such as reading, music, dancing, hunting, and sports. These skills built up his self-esteem. He discovered that silence was not necessarily submission and that self-control was not fear.

He acknowledged that Richard Wright had influenced his writing, but so had T. S. Eliot, Hemingway, Malraux, Dostoyevsky, and Faulkner. Ellison believed the African-American novelist should not "draw his blackness tightly around him . . . nor should the white reader draw his whiteness around himself."

In 1967, Ellison lectured on "The Novel as a Function

of American Democracy." He began by saying that writing novels was "the damnedest thing I ever got into." Ellison said that Americans needed novels to expand their vision of an ideal, democratic society, and he urged writers in his audience to weave three strands into their plots: events from the past to illuminate the present, American ideals of liberty and equality, and moral dilemmas that confront the nation.

Ellison then traced the development of the novel from the eighteenth century to modern times. Early novels like *Robinson Crusoe* portray unique characters forced to adapt to a different environment and to develop new customs and values. Nineteenth-century American novels added a psychological dimension to characterization, for example Melville's *Moby Dick* and Hawthorne's *The Scarlet Letter*. Mark Twain's *The Adventures of Huckleberry Finn* and Stephen Crane's *Red Badge of Courage* added discussion of civil rights and moral issues.

Ellison closed by saying that modern novelists seemed reluctant to portray the complexity and diversity of life in America. Most white fiction writers ignored blacks' contributions to the American experience. Black characters were either left out or portrayed as one-sided, flat, stereotypes. This distorted a realistic picture of American culture.

Editors kept asking Ellison about his second novel-in-progress, which he claimed was a "mythic saga of race and identity, language and kinship in the American experience." He told Albert Murray that he was almost finished with part one of three volumes that would include excerpts from "sermons, folktales, blues, the dozens, swing, and jazz," but said that "the rest was coming slow like my first pair of long pants."

To get the sound of his words right, Ellison tape-recorded himself reading passages and played them back. He particularly enjoyed reading the dialogue of a character named Hickman, a black preacher. It evoked childhood memories of "foot stomping and fanning ladies in long white dresses and sweating elders swaying in the front rows."

On November 29, 1967, the Ellisons were at their summer home in Plainfield, New York. Ralph had nearly finished his second novel. He was laboring over transitional problems and places where he had spoken for the characters rather than allowing them to speak for themselves. While the Ellisons were away for the day, the house caught fire. Most of their belongings were destroyed. Most tragically, 350 pages of the manuscript were burned. Three excerpts were salvaged: "The Roof, the Steeple, and the People," "Juneteenth," and "Night-Talk." Ellison was devastated. He tried to reconstruct his work but soon sank into depression and wrote slowly.

Because he was the author of a classic American novel and a popular critic and essayist, Ellison was invited to speak at numerous university graduations and conferences. He described his lecture schedule as a series of one-night stands. His fee was $175 plus trans-

Ellison (back row, second from left) *poses with fellow recipients of honorary degrees from Harvard University on June 14, 1974. Harvard University president Derek Bok sits front row center.* (AP Photo)

portation. Many black college students were not impressed with Ellison. They felt he lacked charisma. He was polite and courteous but disliked spending time with students who he felt were not willing to work hard. Ellison wrote Murray that "students are ignorant about literature and life—the men wear beards, the girls go braless in their low cut blouses, and they all chew bubble gum."

In 1975, Ellison was elected to the American Academy of Arts and Letters. This was a great honor and in many ways the culmination of his career as a writer. However, he regarded the opening of the Ralph Ellison Library in Oklahoma City as a greater honor. Among friends and dignitaries at the ceremony were State Representative Hannah Atkins, a civil rights activist; Clara Luper, who in 1958 had led the first "sit-in" at a lunch counter in Oklahoma City; and his old friend Jimmy Stewart. In his speech, he reminisced about his love of books and how reading during his childhood had influenced him to become a writer. He urged library administrators and patrons to make the Ralph Ellison Library a place where children could experience imaginative adventures. He thanked the teachers and role models who had introduced him to literature and music.

At the event, a bronze sculpture of Ellison's face was unveiled. The library board had sold the old Dunbar Library property to pay for it. Artist Edward N. Wilson anxiously awaited Ellison's reaction. During the ceremony, Ellison's face remained an impassive mask, and Wilson was crestfallen. Actually, Ellison's stoic expression hid deep emotion. At the reception, he expressed gratitude and asked Wilson for a copy of the sculpture. Like Heraclitus, the Greek philosopher, Ellison believed that "geography is fate." He never forgot his boyhood in Oklahoma, where he acquired the "cold, Oklahoma Negro eye" through which he viewed the rest of the world.

In 1977, John F. Callahan wrote his dissertation "Historic Frequencies of Ralph Waldo Ellison." The title was based on the final scene of *Invisible Man*, in which the narrator says, "Who knows but that, on the lower frequencies, I speak for you?"—meaning that he speaks for outsiders, those who are alienated from society and struggle to find a personal identity. Callahan, who considered Ellison to be the greatest essayist of the twentieth century, invited him to come by for a chat. Their first conversation was awkward, but soon they became good friends. Later, Callahan served as Ellison's literary executor.

In 1986, Random House published *Going to the Territory*, a sixteen-piece collection of Ellison's lectures, memoirs, interviews, and essays, all written after 1964. The title alludes to Huckleberry Finn's final statement, "I got to light out for the territory," the Oklahoma Territory, where Huck hoped to find freedom from social restrictions and encounter "infinite possibilities."

Ellison's goal as a writer had been to submerge his readers below the surface of racial differences to the level of common human experience. His essay "The Little Man at Chehaw Station" explained his belief in diversity. Early immigrants to America had tried to maintain their cultural ethnicities from Europe, Africa, Asia, and the Latin countries with language, clothing, religion, and rituals, but there was also diversity within races, regions, and religions. Inevitably the elements from many cultures were eventually tossed into a common "pot," and a new American identity emerged.

In 1994, at age eighty, Ellison was diagnosed with pancreatic cancer. Realizing his death was imminent, Fanny asked that he be moved from the hospital to their apartment. She notified Callahan, then a professor of humanities at Lewis and Clark College in Portland, Oregon. Ellison instructed Fanny and Callahan to organize his papers and turn them over to the Library of Congress.

Fanny knew that music would comfort Ralph during his last hours, but she could not operate the complicated stereo system he had built. Callahan bought a boom box and some disks by Prokofiev and Louis Armstrong. With closed eyes, Ellison smiled and signaled his approval.

Ralph Waldo Ellison died on April 16, 1994. William Styron, a writer and personal friend, spoke briefly at a graveside service at Trinity Cemetery in New York City. Ellison's obituary in the *New York Times* said he would be remembered as a writer who had a universal reach. Authors Kurt Vonnegut and Joseph Heller acknowledged Ellison's influence on their work.

Fanny Ellison asked Callahan to inventory Ralph's papers and finish the *Juneteenth* novel he had worked on for over forty years. Callahan was astounded by the enormous quantity of books, papers, notes, newspaper clippings, computer disks, and manila file folders piled high in Ellison's office. He began by assembling and editing *The Collected Essays of Ralph Ellison*, which included *Shadow and Act* and *Going to the Territory*. Ellison's old friend Saul Bellow, who won the Nobel Prize for Literature in 1976, wrote the preface.

From under the dining-room table, Fanny dragged out a box that contained folders marked "Early Stories." From these crumbling, yellowed remnants, Callahan pieced together thirteen short stories that were published in a volume entitled *Flying Home and Other Stories* in 1998. Five had never been published before.

Callahan's biggest challenge was the unfinished novel, *Juneteenth*. The title refers to June 19, 1865, when news of the Emancipation Proclamation reached Texas and slaves in that state were freed. In some parts of the South, Juneteenth continues to be a day of celebration, much like July 4. The setting of the novel is America in the 1950s. The characters include Alonzo Hickman, a black evangelist and jazz trombonist, and Adam Sunraider, a white, racist senator from New England. After Sunraider is shot on the floor of the Senate and is dying, he calls for Hickman. Through flashbacks and monologues, their father-son relationship is revealed.

Ellison left 2,000 pages of the manuscript, which included eight previously published episodes: "And Hickman Arrives" (1960), "The Roof, the Steeple and the People" (1960), "It Always Breaks Out" (1963), "Juneteenth" (1965), "Night-Talk" (1969), "A Song of Innocence" (1970), "Cadillac Flambé" (1973), and "Backwhacking: A Plea to the Senator" (1977). The rest consisted of revised episodes and notes he had jotted down on the backs of envelopes and bills.

One episode, "Cadillac Flambé," is about a jazz bass-ist, Lee Willie Minifee, who is listening to the radio in his new white Cadillac convertible as he returns home from a gig. The car symbolizes Minifee's independence, his rise from poverty and obscurity to financial and artistic success. On the radio, Lee Willie hears Senator Sunraider call his new car a "Coon Cage Eight." Minifee decides to make an issue of the Senator's insulting

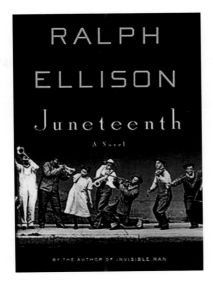

The jacket cover of Ellison's posthumously published novel, Juneteenth.

remark. In a sacrificial act, he sets fire to the Cadillac on the senator's lawn near the nation's capital. While the car burns and crowds gather, Minifee preaches a sermon on the senator's hypocrisy. He laughs as the police carry him away in a straitjacket.

Callahan struggled with how to publish the unfinished novel. He could piece it together, as Ellison had left it, or he could revise and edit it to produce a more finished book. Callahan decided to piece the plot together from the chapters and notes he found in Ellison's office. The result is a tragicomic novel without transitions and many unexplained details about the characters. Critics speculated that Ellison did not finish the novel because he could not find a way to resolve the conflict without making an overt political statement, something he refused to do.

In 2000, the letters Ralph Ellison and Albert Murray

had exchanged between the years 1950 and 1960 were published as *Trading Twelves*. The title refers to "playing the dozens," a game in which participants exchange witty remarks and sarcasm. Ellison's gossipy, conversational tone and informal language reveal a personality not apparent in his formal essays. The two friends conversed "on the lower frequencies," that is, their tone was confidential and candid. The two shared gossip about faculty members at Tuskegee and agreed that the writing of the "hipsters" Norman Mailer, Jack Kerouac, and Bernie Wolfe showed a preoccupation with sex. Ellison said that most African Americans had "more life in [their] toenails than those zombies." They exchanged ideas and critiques for stories and made plans for trips.

In 2002, the Public Broadcasting System (PBS) made a documentary: "Ralph Ellison: An American Journey." It included readings from *Invisible Man* and *Juneteenth*, as well as scenes from Ellison's life in Oklahoma City, Tuskegee, and New York City. In 2003, the Oklahoma City Metropolitan Library celebrated the fiftieth anniversary of the publication of *Invisible Man*, and Ellison was inducted posthumously into the Oklahoma Hall of Fame. The Oklahoma Arts Council commissioned the performance of a one-act play about Ellison by Morris McCorvey. In May 2003, a monument in Riverside Park in Harlem was dedicated to his memory. The large bronze sculpture by Elizabeth Catlett was inspired by *Invisible Man*.

By the end of his life, Ralph Ellison had achieved his boyhood dream of becoming a Renaissance man with

Elizabeth Catlett's bronze sculpture honoring Ellison's concept of the invisible man is situated in Riverside Park in Harlem, overlooking the Hudson River at 150th Street near the Beaumont apartment building where Ellison lived and worked for many years before his death.

skill in diverse and complex arts. In addition to having an encyclopedic knowledge of literature, he had written two novels and numerous essays about literature, folklore, jazz, and blues, all based on his observations of African-American culture. He was a talented dancer. He knew about guns and hunting, sports, electronics, and photography. He was a gourmet cook, an expert on textiles and fashion, and he grew African violets that bloomed prolifically. His imagination knew no limits. He was free to express his individuality and experiences as an African-American citizen of the United States without restraint. He was no longer an invisible man.

TIMELINE

1914	Ralph Waldo Ellison is born March 1.
1917	Lewis Ellison dies. Ida and family move to the parsonage of Avery Chapel African Methodist Episcopal Church.
1931	Graduates from Frederick Douglass High School.
1933	Rides freight train to Tuskegee, Alabama, to study music on scholarship at Tuskegee Institute.
1936	Drops out of school for lack of funds; goes to New York City, studies sculpture, works at the YMCA, meets Langston Hughes and Richard Wright.
1937	Mother dies in Ohio.
1938	Employed as writer with Federal Writers' Project, sponsored by the WPA.
1942	Becomes managing editor of the *Negro Quarterly*.
1943	Enlists in Merchant Marine.
1944	Receives Rosenwald Foundation award to write novel; "King of the Bingo Game" published.
1945	Begins writing *Invisible Man*.
1946	Marries Fanny McConnell.
1952	*Invisible Man* published by Random House.
1953	*Invisible Man* wins National Book Award and Russwurm Award.
1955	Lives in Rome as Fellow of American Academy of Arts & Letters.
1958	Teaches literature at Bard College.
1960	Publishes "And Hickman Arrives."
1961	Alexander White Visiting Professor at University of Chicago.
1962	Teaches creative writing at Rutgers.
1964	American Studies Fellow at Yale; publishes *Shadow and Act*.
1965	Appointed to National Council of Arts and Humanities.

1967	Trustee at the John F. Kennedy Center for the Performing Arts; manuscript of second novel lost in fire at summer home in New York; appointed to Carnegie Commission on Public Television.
1969	Medal of Freedom awarded by President Lyndon B. Johnson.
1970	Awarded France's Chevalier de l'Ordre des Artes et Lettres, presented by Andre Malraux; Albert Schweitzer Professor of Humanities at New York University.
1975	Ralph Ellison Library opens in Oklahoma City; elected to American Academy of Arts and Letters.
1985	Receives National Medal of Arts.
1986	Publishes *Going to the Territory,* a collection of essays, speeches, and reviews.
1994	Dies of pancreatic cancer on April 16 in New York City.
1999	*Juneteenth* is published posthumously.

SOURCES

CHAPTER ONE: Cold Oklahoma Negro Eye

p. 12, "a jackass hiccupping . . ." Ralph Ellison, *Shadow and Act* (New York: Random House, 1964), 191.

p. 12, "farewell to day . . ." Ibid.

p. 19, "These white folks think . . ." Ralph Ellison, *Going to the Territory* (New York: Random House, 1986), 166.

p. 20, "world in which you . . ." Ralph Ellison, *The Collected Essays of Ralph Ellison,* edited by John Callahan (New York: Modern Library, 1995), 6.

p. 23, "bandy-legged, hawk-nosed . . ." Ibid., 454.

p. 24, "What do you think . . ." Ellison, *Going,* 118.

p. 27, "I am not an African . . ." Lawrence Jackson, *Ralph Ellison: Emergence of Genius* (New York: John Wiley & Sons, Inc., 2002), 51.

p. 29, "cold, Oklahoma Negro eye . . ." Ellison, *Collected Essays,* xix.

CHAPTER TWO: Jazz in Deep Deuce

p. 30, "freewheeling, caterwauling . . ." Jackson, *Ralph Ellison,* 66.

p. 32, "blues-driven stomp music . . ." Ibid., 67.

p. 32-33, "like a blue flame in the dark . . ." Ellison, *The Collected Essays,* 273.

CHAPTER THREE: Tuskegee Institute

p. 43, "industrious and a very . . ." Jackson, *Ralph Ellison,* 88.

p. 48, "Negro . . . cheerful and buoyant . . ." Jackson, *Ralph Ellison,* 102.

CHAPTER FOUR: Harlem

p. 56, "Allow them to pay . . ." Jackson, *Ralph Ellison,* 166.

p. 61, "I blundered into it," Ellison, *Shadow,* 14.

p. 62, "partying, boogying . . ." Jackson, *Ralph Ellison,* 172.

p. 62, "the end of [my] childhood," Ibid., 191.

CHAPTER FIVE: The Apprentice

p. 68, "condescension, patronage . . ." Jackson, *Ralph Ellison,* 206.

p. 70, "Blues-toned laughter . . ." Ellison, *Invisible Man,* xvi.

p. 70, "a collage of a nation . . ." Ellison, *The Collected Essays,* xvii.

p. 70, "the mystery . . ." Ibid., 835.

p. 74, "no one here seems . . ." Jackson, *Ralph Ellison,* 228.

p. 74, "That's my stuff!" Ibid., 222.

CHAPTER SIX: A Changing World, A Changing Life

p. 82-83, "evaluate [their] experiences . . ." Ellison, *The Collected Essays,* xxii.

p. 83, "intellectual democracy," Jackson, *Ralph Ellison,* 273.

p. 88, "When I came out . . ." Ibid., 291.

p. 89, "Wright is by himself . . ." Jackson, *Ralph Ellison,* 317.

p. 89, "uniqueness and spiritual unity . . ." Margaret Walker, *Richard Wright: Daemonic Genius* (New York: Warner Books, 1988), 216.

p. 91, "with an infinite capacity . . ." Ellison, *Going,* 49.

CHAPTER SEVEN: The Invisible Becomes Visible

p. 93, "Shut up! Shut up!" Ellison, *Shadow,* 190.

p. 93, "bounced, ricocheted . . ." Ibid.

p. 96, "some kinda sweetback . . ." Ellison, *Invisible Man,* ix.

p. 96, "blues-toned laughter," Ibid., xvi.

p. 97, "purpose, passion, and . . ." Ibid., 353.

p. 99, "did protest the agony of . . ." Ellison, *Going,* 62.

p. 100, "innocence, human error . . ." Ellison, *Shadow,* 177.

p. 100, "naturalism, expressionism . . ." Ibid., 178-179.

p. 100, "Well, let's put it . . ." Ellison, *Going,* 57.

p. 101, "a big fat ole . . ." Albert Murray and Ralph Ellison, *Trading Twelves* (New York: Random House, 2000), 21.

p. 101, "wild starburst . . ." Ellison, *Invisible Man,* xxiii.

p. 103, "vicious distortion of Negro . . ." Jackson, *Ralph Ellison,* 437.

p. 103, "Marvelous refers to . . ." Ellison, *Shadow,* 20.

CHAPTER EIGHT: Applause and Nostalgia

p. 106, "folk, Biblical, scientific . . .." Ellison, *Shadow,* 103.

p. 109, "If I wrote the book . . ." Jackson, *Ralph Ellison,* 420.

p. 110, "Mose [was] living . . ." Murray and Ellison, *Trading,* 51.

p. 111, "raw, red clay mounds . . ." Ibid., 61.

p. 111, "red-cock crowing . . ." Jackson, *Ralph Ellison,* vii.

p. 111, "living in that earlier . . ." Murray and Ellison, *Trading,* 61.

p. 111, "I've got one Oklahoma . . ." Ellison, *Juneteenth,* xi.

CHAPTER NINE: Change the Joke and Slip the Yoke

p. 112, "give Rome back to . . ." Murray and Ellison, *Trading,* 103.

p. 114, "cornbread, sweet potatoes . . ." Ibid., 118.

p. 115, "irrational social change . . . social conflicts," Ellison, *Going,* 246.

p. 115, "How did they escape . . ." Ibid., 299.

p. 117, "comic catharsis," Ellison, *Shadow,* 64.

p. 117-118, "The smart man . . ." Ibid., 70.

p. 118, "long, loud rant . . ." Ibid., 72.

p. 119, "dance the chicks . . ." Ralph Ellison, *Living With Music,* edited by Robert G. O'Meally (New York: Modern Library, 2001), 250.

p. 120, "a black Jew," Ellison, *Collected Essays,* 363.

p. 120, "All us old-fashioned . . ." Ibid.

p. 121, "makes life swing," Ellison, *Living,* ix.

p. 122, "vital covenant . . ." Ellison, *Going,* 330.

p. 122, "crack in the Liberty Bell . . ." Ibid., 332.

p. 123, "talked a lot . . . barbershop rhetoric," Ellison, *Living,* 280.

p. 124, "That just proves . . ." Ellison, *The Collected Essays,* 359.

p. 124, "dissolve the barriers . . ." Ellison, *Going,* 291.

CHAPTER TEN: Jazz

p. 126, "It was a place that . . ." Ellison, *Shadow,* 202.

p. 126, "apprenticeships, ordeals . . ." Ibid., 208.

p. 126-127, "history [of modern jazz is] a tall tale . . ." Ellison, *Living,* 51.

p. 127, "musical instruments were . . ." Ibid, 52-55.

p. 127, "the real secret of . . ." Ibid., 140.

p. 129, "mechanistic, repetitive, nervous . . ." Ellison, *Shadow,* 203.

p. 129, "fragmented, chaotic . . ." Ellison, *Living,* 51.

p. 129, "What kind of 'bird' . . ." Ibid., 75.

p. 130, "The cats have . . ." Murray and Ellison, *Trading,* 193.

p. 130, "the frantic shriek . . ." Ellison, *Living,* xxviii.

p. 130, "gave even the . . ." Ibid., 120.

p. 131, "styles of dancing . . ." Ibid., xxxii.

p. 131, "There is no Blues School," Jackson, *Ralph Ellison,* 342.

p. 131, "impulse to keep painful . . ."Ellison, *Shadow,* 90.

p. 131-132, "enigmatic, smiling mask," Ibid., 77.

CHAPTER ELEVEN: *Juneteenth*

p. 136, "celebrate human life . . ." Ellison, *Shadow,* 114.

p. 136, "an opaque steel jug . . ." Ibid., 116.

p. 137, "draw his blackness . . ." Ibid., 170.

p. 138, "the damnedest thing . . ." Ellison, *Going,* 308.

p. 138-139, "mythic saga of race . . ." Ellison, *Juneteenth,* xiii.

p. 139, "sermons, folktales . . ." Ibid., xv.

p. 139, "the rest was . . ." Murray and Ellison, *Trading,* 67.

p. 139, "foot stomping and . . ." Ellison, *The Collected Essays,* 388.

p. 140, "students are ignorant . . ." Murray and Ellison, *Trading,* 204.

p. 141, "geography is fate," Ellison, *The Collected Essays,* xviii.

p. 141, "cold, Oklahoma Negro eye . . ." Ibid., xix.

p. 146, "more life in his toenails...." Murray and Ellison, *Trading,* 68.

BIBLIOGRAPHY

Bloom, Harold, ed. *Ralph Ellison's* Invisible Man. Philadelphia: Chelsea House, 1999.

Burke, Bob and Denyvetta Davis. *Ralph Ellison: A Biography.* Oklahoma Heritage Association, 2003.

Chapman, Abraham, ed. *New Black Voices.* New York: New American Library, 1972.

Devlin, Jeanne. "50 Years of the Invisible Man." *Metro Library.* Oklahoma City: Metropolitan Library System, January 2002.

Devlin, Jeanne. "Ralph Ellison: The Oklahoma Days." *Metro Library.* Oklahoma City: Metropolitan Library System, March 2002.

Eliot, Thomas S. *The Waste Land and Other Poems.* New York: Signet Classics, 1997.

Ellison, Ralph. *The Collected Essays of Ralph Ellison.* John F. Callahan, ed. New York: Modern Library, 1995.

————. *Flying Home and Other Stories.* John Callahan, ed. New York: Random House, 1996.

————. *Going to the Territory.* New York: Random House, 1986.

————. *Invisible Man.* New York: Vintage Books, 1980.

————. *Juneteenth.* John Callahan, ed. New York: Random House, 1999.

————. *Living With Music.* Robert G. O'Meally, ed. New York: Modern Library, 2001.

———. *Shadow and Act.* New York: Random House, 1964.

Hentoff, Nat. "Jazz Is Coming Home to Harlem." *Wall Street Journal.* March 18, 2004.

"Invisible No More." *Metro Library.* Oklahoma City: Metropolitan Library System, 2002.

Hughes, Langston. *The Collected Poems of Langston Hughes.* Rampersad, Arnold and David Roessel, eds. New York: Vintage Classics, 1995.

Jackson, Lawrence. *Ralph Ellison: Emergence of Genius.* New York: John Wiley & Sons, 2002.

Murray, Albert and Ralph Ellison. *Trading Twelves.* John Callahan, ed. New York: Random House, 2000.

Parks, Gordon. *Voices in the Mirror.* New York: Doubleday, 1990.

Rhynes, Martha. *I, Too, Sing America: The Life of Langston Hughes.* Greensboro: Morgan Reynolds, 2002.

Walker, Margaret. *Richard Wright: Daemonic Genius.* New York: Warner Books, 1988.

WEB SITES

http://www.pbs.org/jazz/
PBS offers a companion site to the documentary film *Jazz* by Ken Burns, with many links, informative articles, and audio samples.

http://www.pbs.org/wnet/americanmasters/database/ ellison_r_homepage.html
A site devoted to Ellison's life and work, containing footage from the American Masters Series documentary about Ralph Ellison and an interview with the filmmaker.

http://www.english.uiuc.edu/maps/poets/s_z/r_wright/ wright_life.htm
A discussion of Richard Wright's life and work.

http://www.pbs.org/wgbh/pages/frontline/shows/race/etc/ road.html
This site, entitled "The Two Nations of Black America," sketches the debate that emerged between two different ways of approaching the issue of race: that advocated by W. E. B. Du Bois and that advocated by Booker T. Washington.

http://www.afro.com/history/tusk/tuskmain.html
A brief history of the Tuskegee Airmen, with links to related articles and to the Afro-American Newspapers online Black History Museum.

INDEX